secret GARDEN *spaces*

JENNIFER POTTER

PLANT DIRECTORY BY
NOËL KINGSBURY

conran
OCTOPUS

*For my son, Robert, and for
Edward Fawcett, who both
inspired a love of secret spaces.*

First published in 1998
under the title of SECRET GARDENS
This edition published in 2002
by Conran Octopus Ltd
a part of the Octopus Publishing Group
2–4 Heron Quays
London E14 4JP
www.conran-octopus.co.uk

Text copyright © Jennifer Potter 1998

Design and layout copyright
© Conran Octopus Ltd 1998

COMMISSIONING EDITOR Stuart Cooper
MANAGING EDITOR Kate Bell
COPY EDITOR Helen Ridge
EDITORIAL ASSISTANT Tanya Robinson
INDEX Hilary Bird

ART EDITOR Isabel de Cordova
PICTURE RESEARCH Helen Fickling
CASE STUDY PLANS Lesley Craig
PRODUCTION Suzanne Sharpless

British Library Cataloguing-in-Publication
Data. A catalogue record for this book
is available from the British Library

ISBN 1-84091-244-8

Printed and bound in China

Page 1: Keyhole views both conceal
and reveal the essence of mystery.
Page 2: Jungle planting creates an
unexpected hideaway in the urban
landscape, lushly serene – explore this
exotic retreat further on pages 120–3.
Page 3: A path snakes into the garden
like the thread of a plot.

INTRODUCTION
6

What Makes a Garden Secret?
Secret Garden History
Design Secrets

HIDDEN ROOMS
20

A Secret Room
A Garden of Many Rooms

CASE STUDY
A Garden of Green Rooms

INTIMATE RETREATS
46

Summerhouses and Pavilions
Gazebos; Arbours, Pergolas,
Tunnels and Bowers

CASE STUDY
A Garden of Many Retreats

URBAN OASES
72

Courtyards
Roof Gardens

CASE STUDY
A Garden in the Sky

INTO THE WILD
98

Woodland Gardens
Clearings and Meadows
Temperate Jungles

CASE STUDY
A Backyard Jungle

GARDENS OF
MAKE-BELIEVE
124

Grottoes
Hideaways and Dens
Treehouses

CASE STUDY
A Treetop Walk

Guarding the Secret 148

Plants for Secret Gardens 149
Index 154
Acknowledgements 156

ABOVE: Enclosure is central to the idea of secret gardens; here circular walls create
a mood of quiet mystery.

INTRODUCTION

A tangled arch stands sentinel at the entrance,

its stonework flaked with age. Memories

stir – of other gardens, other footsteps that have

been here before you. Time rustles as you

hesitate; and your heart beats faster.

Secret gardens dig deep into the psyche. From childhood, we carry images of enchanted space, like Sleeping Beauty's castle, ringed by a wall of thorns until the young prince breaks the spell. Discovering a lost paradise is another powerful 'myth' that has its roots in religious symbolism. (We are all searching for Eden.) Literature, too, offers models that make us long for secret spaces of our own. In Secret Garden Spaces, Frances Hodgson Burnett's classic tale of Edwardian England, the orphan Mary re-awakens a lost, locked garden hidden behind high walls. Equally magical is the crumbling château discovered by the hero of Alain-Fournier's Le Grand Meaulnes, inhabited by children and invaded by bushes run wild. Stories like these continue to resonate throughout adult life in dreams of a place apart – a secret paradise that refreshes the spirits as well as the senses, a place to which you alone hold the key...

RIGHT: The entrance to an abandoned pleasure park quickens the spirit with echoes of a lost world crying out for rediscovery.

WHAT MAKES A GARDEN SECRET?

Though each secret garden is secret in its own way – and each individual subscribes to different mysteries – let me suggest three qualities essential for all. The first is concealment, which usually means enclosure. A secret is something hidden, shut away, concealed from all but the initiated. 'If I tell you about my garden, it won't be secret any more, will it?' How often did I hear these words while writing this book?

A secret garden must also – and just as obviously – be private, reserved for the enjoyment of a person, a clan, a group, or others of your choosing. Ownership is not the issue – even public gardens have their own private spaces. Implying privacy is an art that owes as much to psychology as to horticulture or architecture.

The third element is mystery, tempting exploration. Often the journey is literal, as you are lured by 'clues' that draw you up the garden path and beyond: the trickle of water offstage, a trellised arch marking the threshold of adventure, a stepping-stone path curving out of view. But sometimes the exploration is internal as you stop to ask yourself why this corner or that sets your pulse racing. I like the strange, the unexpected, the familiar turned inside out like a well-worn sleeve. 'You will move into the garden as into the "otherness" of an unknown place,' wrote Russell Page in *The Education of a Gardener*. I'm tagging close to his heels.

FAR LEFT:
Blocks of clipped
hedging form
interlocking
compartments
in the garden of
a Spanish villa,
complicating its
geometry and
adding an element
of suspense.

LEFT: Stillness
deepens the mystery
of this American
garden, where
a pensive bust,
reflected columns
and melancholic
cypresses achieve
the timelessness
of dreams.

SECRET GARDEN HISTORY

Gardens began, I believe, to celebrate divine mysteries. The first examples included the temple gardens of Ancient Egypt, and the sacred groves of Ancient Greece set with shrines and planted with shady trees and species dedicated to resident deities: oak for Zeus, laurel (bay) for Apollo, ivy for Dionysus. Entry to these groves was forbidden to all except the initiated.

Though I can't claim acquaintance with the original, I have stepped into a modern equivalent: a grassy clearing banked with rhododendrons in the Otterlo hunting forest of the eastern Netherlands. Here, in the Kröller-Müller sculpture park, I was looking for an installation by the Scottish sculptor, artist and gardener Ian Hamilton Finlay; 'Five columns for the Kröller-Müller' was the only name I knew.

Despite my map, the path was difficult to find. None of the strangers I stopped to ask knew where it was. On the point of giving up the search, I pushed my way through rhododendron bushes and emerged unexpectedly into a grassy glade, eerily still. A handful of oaks and a Scots pine defined the edges of the clearing, their bases encircled with stone plinths like

RIGHT: Wilful cunning has created a garden of keyhole views and dislocated spaces. This fountain enclosed between hedges and Boston ivy can be heard but not always seen.

LEFT: Equally suited to formal elegance and ragged abandon, trellis work has been used since the sixteenth century to define secret corners – as private in feel as they are exposed in fact.

Graeco-Roman columns. It looked and felt like the scene of a crime – a place of ritual sacrifice at least. Only later did I discover that 'Sacred Grove' is its usual name.

But 'secret' does not always mean 'scary'. Two traditions in particular owe their inspiration to very different interpretations of secrecy – Ancient China and Islam. Mirroring the totality of the universe, Chinese gardens offer the visitor a labyrinth of winding paths and courtyards stacked one within the other, each subdivision linked with partial views and teasing suggestions that confuse time and space. The courtyard gardens of Islam, by contrast, re-work the same designs over and over again, enfolding the faithful in an earthly paradise of spreading shade, gently flowing fountains, fragrance and cool pavilions. Their secrets lie in seclusion and in their denial of the blistering heat and dust beyond the walls. Such a vision of paradise spread swiftly into Moorish Spain and southern Europe, into Hispanic California and the rest of the Americas, wherever transcendental man ventured into the stony desert.

RIGHT: Crossing boundaries needs special thought. Stone steps, monumental urns and curious lions here mark the transition from formal to wild like a rite of passage.

If the Islamic idea of paradise comes out of a very specific climate and culture, the notion of the garden as a place of refuge and contemplation criss-crosses the ages and the continents. From the cloisters and fenced 'flowery meads' of medieval Europe to the raked gravel seas of fifteenth-century Japan, the garden wall shuts out the hostile, clamouring world. When fashionable melancholia swept Europe in the seventeenth century, the rage was for tree-house retreats. In mid century, the diarist and scholar John Evelyn built himself 'a little study over a Cascade, to pursue my Melancholy houres shaded there with Trees, & Silent Enough.' The urge is just as strong today.

And so, among the rooftops and pinched backyards of our cities, beyond the showy lawns and borders of gardens everywhere, we continue to erect 'shadowhouses' like these – private spaces to enact private dreams, whatever those dreams might be.

The *giardino segreto* of the Italian Renaissance came from the same urge for privacy and retirement. Often placed near the main house or villa, these gardens were not so much hidden as exclusive in their privileges. As a lesser person, you might be able to wander at will through the grander, public areas of the garden but the secret garden was reserved, strictly, for the owner's family and chosen guests. In highly structured societies,

of his jealous queen. Later sources suggest he placed the bower at the centre of a complicated labyrinth. But the romance of bowers, summerhouses, arbours and pavilions is engrained in cultures the world over: Ottoman kiosks or tents, Hindu *baradaris*, Mogul pavilions, Chinese tea-houses, gothic octagons, rustic root-houses, latticed pagodas and peacock swings, French *gloriettes* and Spanish *glorietas* (both words a translation of the Arabic word for 'glorious'). Even the names are evocative of long, lazy afternoons spent drowsing in the burnished heat, or of dalliance under a summer's moon.

Wildness is another side to secrecy: a quality that, like beauty, shifts its definition down the ages. The 'wildernesses' of seventeenth-century Europe were clipped and formal affairs, with intersecting paths flanked by hedges offering jaded courtiers and gentlefolk the prospect (though not the reality) of getting lost in the wood. Like pilgrims, their eventual progress was assured. Then the woods grew slowly wilder, especially in North America where the clearing in the forest became a symbol of a pioneer past. Yet as the real wilderness recedes, our yearning for 'nature' and 'wildness' has intensified. A paradox, perhaps, but in an increasingly man-made environment, we ask the natural world to give us back a sense of who we are.

Secret gardens stand on the margin between the wild and the tamed – that's why they matter so much in the hard-edged world of today. Although their traditions stretch back across cultures and centuries, they remain as potent now as they ever were. Echoes, hints, allusions add to the mystery, taking us into worlds where nothing is quite what it seems, and where the remembered and the invented become confused. And so the final chapter looks at gardens of make-believe: grottoes, treehouses, dens for adults and children, flights of fancy that slip through the chink between the known and the unknown, inviting us on a journey that will take us out of ourselves.

such as Mogul Asia, the exclusion went further, creating whole terraces or enclosures for high-caste women only, like the uppermost terrace of Nishat Bagh, Kashmir, with its three-storied gazebos and wondrous views. At Lahore Fort, Pakistan, ladies of the harem could wander among the orange trees and heady scents of their own garden, the Paien Bagh.

Intimacy is a feature of all these gardens – intimacy with God, nature, family, friends or self. Inevitably, stories hint at scandals, at secret assignations. Near the royal hunting park at Woodstock, in Oxfordshire, Henry II is reputed to have hidden his mistress, the 'fair Rosamund', in a bower to save her from the wrath

'Footfalls echo in the memory
Down the passage which we did not take
Towards the door we never opened
Into the rose-garden.'
T. S. ELIOT, 'THE FOUR QUARTETS'

DESIGN SECRETS

Garden-making is like story-telling. I write stories to make people turn the page and I make gardens to encourage people to turn the corner, and entice them to the end.

Patience, receptivity and diligence are the qualities you must cultivate to let a garden grow of its own accord – the same requirements you need to make a book or a painting. Some of the best garden-makers and landscape architects borrow freely from other disciplines – painting, drawing and sculpture in particular. The late Sir Geoffrey Jellicoe, for example, proposed this exercise in composition: 'You, the landscape designer, have been asked to design a "giardino segreto" in an existing woodland glade through which runs a rivulet … Suddenly you pause before a Picasso plate. Something has stirred within you. By all means take note that it shows a woman's face, but what has held you is the beautiful abstract composition. Your imagination now converts it into a woodland-garden scene …'

Something has stirred within you … I hope this book might achieve a similar effect. Before you start planning and planting, give your garden time to communicate its own requirements. See how the light filters around the garden. Watch the rain as it falls and get acquainted with your soil and your surroundings, the sights and sounds and smell of the place. Talk to the trees, if you must.

Think carefully, too, about how you want the space to be used. Secret gardens, by their nature, are quiet places, removed from the noise and stress of everyday lives. But calm and peace are not the only qualities on offer here. Strangeness and danger, magic and make-believe, containment and escape are all aspects of secrecy this book sets out to explore.

The garden as narrative journey is a constant theme; the mystery story in particular has much to offer the gardener with its opposing principles of surprise or suspense.

'Let not each beauty ev'ry where be spy'd,
Where half the skill is decently to hide.'

So said Alexander Pope in the eighteenth century and garden-makers are repeating his refrain just as heartily today. Though the unexpected becomes expected over time, surprise as a principle helps to keep a garden fresh – and helps to stop the garden taking itself too seriously. 'This landscape is like the face you overlook,' wrote filmmaker Derek Jarman about his own patch of Kent shingle, 'the face of an angel with a naughty smile.' The Chinese in particular understood the value of sudden shocks, with moon-shaped openings cut into garden walls, and latticed windows giving an unexpected glimpse into the courtyard beyond. Sculpture, ornament, found objects and unusual planting can all introduce the unexpected to lift the spirits.

Suspense is even more compelling as a way of drawing others into the recesses of your imagination. Paths suggest the excitement of a journey, especially ones that wind out of view. 'In a path is the beginning of narrative, that sure and welcoming sign of human presence,' wrote American Michael Pollan in *Second Nature*. But paths lead equally towards the unknown. Doorways, gates, sudden gaps in the hedge are like hooks in the plot. Who can see a half-open doorway in a tall brick wall without pushing through to see what lies on the other side? A summer scent of unseen philadelphus or giant lily can drive a person wild, as can the spurt of distant fountains. The playful gardener scatters 'clues' like these to draw people on – and sometimes to confound their expectations.

In a flint-walled garden near Oxford, constructed as a series of rooms-within-rooms, I once followed the sound of splashing water to its source (or so I thought), into the next compartment and down an avenue of rosa mundi. I should have paid more attention. The sound I heard first was a steady splash, while the fountain

FAR LEFT: This cutaway view at the Villa Noailles, Grasse, frames the hidden peony garden with its column copied from the Villa Aldobrandini, Frascati, and helps to 'borrow' the distant landscape.

LEFT: Squeezed between tall, clipped hedges, a path transforms the garden into a labyrinth.

RIGHT: A secret garden needs a destination worth the journey. Here the path leads through crooked trees and thickly clumped hostas towards a shady bower.

I found lapped gently over the brim like the cups of paradise. And so I nearly missed the innermost secret of all: a garden of cherry trees planted within the roofless walls of a ruined barn, where water from a curlicued spout splashed into an old stone bath.

Concealment and enclosure – so central to the theme of this book – are covered in more detail later on. For a garden, the ideal is to create an aura of privacy without claustrophobia, and without casting your garden into gloomiest shade. It is possible to imply concealment without cutting off sight lines – an open arbour, for example, can *feel* the most desperately private of places. Walls, too, can be used to create ambiguous spaces where the boundaries appear to slide round distant views, making the hills your own. Even the great *bosquets* or thickets of Versailles have hidden corners, where the tyranny of geometry gives way to a leafy stillness.

All narratives (and all gardens) have to end somewhere, and mysteries, in particular, require some resolution, some point if they are to be more than shaggy dog stories. I certainly don't mean to imply that every thread should be neatly unravelled. But the final destination, the 'heart' of the secret garden, must make its exploration worthwhile. Later chapters are full of examples of how this may be done: through planting or the creation of special features to intensify the experience – water, grottoes, sculpture or sculpted plants, for example. Sometimes all that is needed is a still, quiet heart.

And finally, once you have made (or found) your secret garden, you need to think how you may safeguard its mystery. Since the Middle Ages, at least, the Egyptian sphinx has guarded the entrance to many grand gardens. In Greek literature, you may remember, the sphinx guarded the tombs at Thebes, devouring those who failed to answer her riddle: 'Which animal has four feet in the morning, two at midday and three in the afternoon?' Like Oedipus, who eventually supplied the answer, this book works its way towards the solution.

Hide your secrets well. I once visited a public garden that boasted its own secret garden, clearly marked on the map. In case I missed it, 'The Secret Garden' was stamped in plastic and hung above an arched doorway that opened on to a scraggy yew and a path that wiggled needlessly round the back. I hope this book will inspire you to do better than that.

ABOVE: Even outdoors, 'rooms' need doorways, walls and anticipated surprises to entice you inside.

HIDDEN ROOMS

Moving deeper into the garden, you find yourself

trapped by a mysterious geometry of man-made

urn and gangly trees. A fountain overflows somewhere

up ahead, and children's laughter echoes out of sight

guiding you to the labyrinth's still heart.

The best gardens, like the best books, are the ones that invite you to read between the lines. They turn and twist, tempting you to explore the byways of their plot and to enter into their subtle mysteries. The hidden rooms of this chapter are of two kinds: first, the secluded corner tucked into the folds of a smaller garden – a place to sit on a summer's evening, perhaps, or a scented enclosure filled with flowers that you discover like a hidden pearl.

The second kind will usually be found in larger gardens of 'rooms-within-rooms', transforming the garden into a journey through different moods, sensations and settings; a series of Chinese boxes whose locks and secrets you must somehow unpick. What lies at the end of the twisting path? A bench is sighted through leaves. Water spills faintly beyond a thickening bamboo. Clues like these draw you on towards an unknown goal.

RIGHT: A line of pleached plane trees marches towards the cut-out view
of the fountain, where a wall of Boston ivy bars your way.

TRADITION

The fashion for gardens planned as a series of outdoor rooms began, like so much else, with the Italian Renaissance when the princes, cardinals and popes of Florence and Rome breached the closed garden walls of medieval Europe. Their sumptuous terraces and palazzos provided a fine setting for strolling like gods through the landscapes of myth and allegory. Near Rome, for example, at the Villa d'Este's Fountain of Dragons, the forking path led to vice or virtue, Venus or Diana.

But even Renaissance princes felt the need to retire from public gaze. The *giardino segreto* was a feature of the grandest palaces. Often sited near the house and overlooked by upper rooms, these gardens were closed rather than hidden, intended for the private use of their owners. If some disappoint with their plainness, others live up to the romance of the name. In her celebrated book *Italian Gardens*, Georgina Masson describes a little walled garden at the sixteenth-century Villa Capponi, near Florence, reached (until this century) only by an underground passage from the house: 'With its flower-filled box parterres, gurgling wall fountain and battlemented walls festooned with roses and wisteria, this little room is probably the most enchanting example of the Italian *giardino segreto* in existence.'

My favourite hides in the hills near Rome, by the casino of the Palazzo Farnese, Caprarola. The winter and summer terraces near the palazzo are – for Italy – unremarkable. But take the grassy path up through the pines and you stumble across one of the most magical secret retreats in all Italy.

FAR LEFT: Italian Renaissance gardens are famed for exhilarating effects. At the Villa d'Este, near Rome, an arcaded path leads behind the thunderous Fountain of the Oval; the Grotto of Venus is nearby.

LEFT: The water parterre at the Villa Gamberaia, Tuscany, shares many of the features of a *giardino segreto*: easy access from the house and the simple materials of stone, water and arched evergreens. Colour (apart from green) is restricted to a few urns of bright pelargoniums.

A dolphin cascade takes the eye up a gentle slope flanked by ramped walls, towards a pair of sternly reclining water giants. Behind them, the casino building rises in honeyed stone from restful greens, the secrets of its terrace guarded by stone caryatids – weird, oversize figures with baskets on their heads. Crossing the threshold is like entering a pagan world.

Though the garden of compartments was supposedly swept aside by the English landscape style of the eighteenth century, many hidden corners remained despite the dictates of style. People *liked* their walled enclosures, and their flowers, and intimacy of scale. And so the ideals of Italian garden design remained potent throughout Europe, re-emerging with the often flamboyant gardens of the Victorians, where 'Art' regained the ascendancy over 'Nature'.

One of the most dramatic of the Victorian gardens is Biddulph Grange in Staffordshire, created in the 1840s and 1850s and now magnificently restored by the National Trust. Planned as a series of interlocking amoebic shapes, the garden uses tunnels, rocks, Chinese doorways and illusionist buildings to draw the visitor into its many mysteries. Pass from the sunlight of the pinetum into the half-timbered Cheshire Cottage, take the left corridor and you emerge from the gloom into Egypt, flanked by pyramidal yews and a pair of guarding sphinxes. Should you fail to stumble on to the tree roots of the Stumpery (many people do), you could miss the greatest secret of all: a high-Victorian vision of China planted with some of the choicest specimens introduced by the great plant hunters such as Robert Fortune.

The twentieth century has seen the taste for gardens planned as outdoor rooms grow ever stronger, despite a gradual shrinking in the size of our plots. On both sides of the Atlantic, the turn-of-the-century Arts and Crafts style of house and garden design encouraged the creation of quiet spaces within the grander plan. In her garden at Munstead Wood, Surrey, for example, Gertrude Jekyll (the *grande dame* of Edwardian gardening) planned for herself a hidden area walled with evergreens, away from any paths, where she grew the quiet flowers of early summer: catmint and London pride, hart's-tongue ferns and Solomon's seal, pansies and irises in pale lilac, the perfumed flowers of the white Himalayan musk rose.

America, too, abounds with 'secret gardens' created in the same spirit – ones like the walled garden at the Rancho Los Alamitos, California, developed in the 1920s by society hostess Florence Green Bixby. Located near the bedroom wing of the house, her secret garden's vine-laden walls enveloped a tiny, sunny space where she looked after her many grandchildren, nephews and nieces, and sought privacy for herself.

A much-loved American example of the garden-rooms style is Dumbarton Oaks in Washington DC, created between the 1920s and 1940s by Beatrix Farrand for Mildred Barnes Bliss and presented in 1941 to Harvard University. Though the hidden

LEFT: The China doorway at Victorian Biddulph Grange, created by James Bateman, shows off his love of dramatic entrances, and of the light-filtering effects of Japanese maples.

OVERLEAF LEFT: Paths that wind out of sight increase the tension of the unknown. Here the path cuts through a rustling thicket of bamboo.

OVERLEAF RIGHT: In larger gardens, avenues of trees create stately links between different areas, defining and enclosing a route without introducing claustrophobia.

bowling green beyond the copse no longer exists, you can still catch a sense of the secret herb garden planned for the wisteria arbour, offering the contrast (in Farrand's own words) 'between sunlight and shade, the sound of falling water, the scent of herbs, the movement of wind and birds'. Farrand herself considered the quietest, most peaceful part of the garden to be the ellipse of box (since replaced with hornbeam) surrounding a simple jet fountain, reached by a steeply sloping box walk.

In England, from the 1930s, Vita Sackville-West and Harold Nicolson reclaimed the gardens of Sissinghurst Castle, Kent, creating one of the most famous English gardens of rooms-within-rooms. Despite the thousands who visit Sissinghurst each year, the intimacy of the gardens continues to enchant. Statues and archways draw you down narrow axial walks that open suddenly into small, geometrical rooms. You find yourself moving constantly from the known into the unknown, enticed by the texture of openings (crumbly Kent brick, especially) and snatches of shapes, colours and heady scents ahead. Changes of level and mood keep the senses aroused as you pass from the straight lines of the pleached lime walk into the ferny wildness of the Nuttery; or step from the sensual overload of the rose garden into the cleansing bare green of the yew circle.

A SECRET ROOM

In planning your own secret garden room, you will need to think first how much space you have to play with, and the kind of 'secret' you wish to inspire. Most urban and suburban gardeners will start with a smallish, regular-shaped plot. The challenge is to break up the space so that it doesn't reveal itself all at once.

In small town plots, say 15 metres (50 feet) in length, the instinct of many gardeners is to site the most secret area away from the house. Venetian gardens, for instance, are usually planned with three well-defined spaces: a formal garden nearest the house, often paved or terraced; a second area set aside for the enjoyment of nature; and a third, the most important area, tucked away at the end, with gazebos and shielded corners designed to be enjoyed alone or in secret meetings with friends. Hidden areas that catch the late afternoon sun will be especially welcome at the end of narrow town gardens.

How you conceal your secret garden will depend on whether you wish to create for yourself a real hideaway, its entrance camouflaged like a secret trapdoor, or whether your intentions are more playful. A path that winds into the darkness of a shrubbery calls out for exploration. Apparently solid planting, provided by clumps of bamboo, thickly planted shrubs, or tall hedges of beech, hornbeam and yew, will deter even the curious, who with luck might not notice that the line is staggered in places, allowing you to slip between the cracks. Some of the most secret gardens of all are reached by tunnels or underground passageways, like escape routes to a priest hole – a hidden rose tunnel leading towards a secret terrace, for example, its entrance concealed by a narrow arch clipped through a tall beech hedge. These are the gardens no one wishes us to see.

Occasionally, even city gardeners are blessed with unusual sites: chalk pits and quarries or L-shaped gardens created by accidents of ownership. These can be very liberating, especially if you disguise the elbow of the 'L'. One way to do this is to cut off the lateral view entirely. The first part of the garden (seen from the house) can be artificially elongated by planting hedges that taper towards a focal point. At the end of this first section, you discover a path leading into the 'secret' part of the L – either directly, or squeezed between further hedges so that the point of entry is delayed until the tip. Another – simpler – approach would be to hint at the existence of the second garden, without giving away too much – using an arch or tunnel angled to block direct sight lines from one space to another. A tangled planting of vines, espaliered fruit, hop and roses can further disguise the opening, while drawing you forward.

Gardens that change level can also make you *feel* very private, even when exposed to view. At the heart of a secluded herb garden in Hampshire, in a slight hollow, the owner has created a sunken serenity garden around a lover's knot of clipped box, the area encircled with sedative and tranquillizer herbs to cheer the melancholy. Here she sits when she wants to be alone. Even when the garden is walked by others, she knows that no one will presume to disturb her. You can use trees to imply privacy in much the same way. A formal planting of pleached or bare-stemmed trees such as hornbeam or lime – in a square or a circle, perhaps, or that most potent of shapes, the ellipse – acts on the mind like a magic circle. Stepping into the centre is like walking into the heart of a charm.

But for 'real' privacy, your hidden room will need to be enclosed. Choose your form of enclosure carefully, as this will largely define the atmosphere of the place you are creating. From childhood reading and dreamings, the stock images of secret gardens are

traditional and deeply romantic. Crumbling brick walls, festoons of ivy and cascading Bourbon roses (white with perhaps the faintest blush of pink) exert an undeniably strong attraction. It is possible, however, to invest modern materials – even 'unromantic' concrete and hard-edged stone – with an aura of secrecy, through wilder planting, for example, or unexpected juxtapositions. In a garden at the Chelsea Flower Show, designer Christopher Bradley-Hole contrasted hard stone walls with a tangle of select cow parsleys and chervil (*Anthriscus sylvestris* 'Ravenswing' and *Chaerophyllum hirsutum* 'Roseum') and unusually tall *Thalictrum rochebruneanum*, backed by a formal line of Italian cypress and a young stone pine. The result was unexpectedly peaceful.

There are many other ways of walling your secret enclosure. Theatrical effects like projecting 'wings' of scenery or manipulated perspective can create an illusion of depth; and depth breeds mystery. Coppiced willow stems planted in bare earth make marvellous tunnels or 'living' screens. Other good screening plants include bamboos, old rhododendrons with their primeval twisted stems, banks of thorny roses, or thickets of trees planted in quincunx fashion like a number five domino. Some of my favourite places are gardened by scavengers skilled at salvaging old columns, balustrades and assorted stonework from demolition sites and using these as room dividers in their

gardens, haphazardly mixed in with exuberant and exotic planting to suggest the romantic decay of old gardens. I think of Ninfa, near Rome, where roses and wisteria bloom among a memory of medieval ruins. And I am a great admirer of the strangeness of formal hedges, especially those of Belgian designer Jacques Wirtz which range from the oddly bulbous to ones chopped and banked into perfect geometric shapes.

Whatever your favoured style of enclosure, pay particular attention to the entrance into your secret garden. The entrance frames a view, marking the threshold to a transformation about to take place. The door in Hodgson Burnett's *The Secret Garden* is always approached with a shiver of excitement, like the first time Mary shows the garden to her new friend, Dickon. 'She led him round the laurel path and to the walk where the ivy grew so thickly. Dickon followed her with a queer, almost pitying, look on his face. He felt as if he were being led to look at some strange bird's nest and must move softly. When she stepped to the wall and lifted the hanging ivy he started. There was a door and Mary pushed it slowly open and they passed in together ...'

Metal gates or grilles set in solid walls both conceal and reveal, creating a tension that draws you inevitably to see what lies beyond, like the latticed windows and pierced doorways of Chinese gardens: moon-shaped openings are especially favoured

FAR LEFT: At Long Barn, Kent (Vita Sackville-West's home before Sissinghurst), a door into the hedge gives surreal meaning to an 'outdoor room'.

CENTRE: The entrance here entices through contrast: the straight edges of path, lawn and hedge versus the rounded bower of trained apple and moon-shaped door.

LEFT: Old brick walls, roses, an open doorway – this classic image of the secret garden plays, too, with the drama of light and shade.

RIGHT: Framing a view gives it added meaning, but take care to mould the picture to its frame. Here woven wicker perfectly suits the nonchalant Cupid rising from a water lily pond.

as the circle, in China, signifies heaven. Sometimes the opening into your secret area is best left wild – just the hint of a path slipping into a bank of evergreen shrubs like box or pittosporum or the Mexican orange blossom (*Choisya ternata*). Alternatively, you may want to mark the opening more distinctly, creating a definite 'door' in the hedge with an archway – or even a real door. But remember Russell Page's advice in *The Education of a Gardener*: 'If you intend to make an enclosed garden, you must plan and plant and build with that idea uppermost; if at any point you decide to open it up in any way, then this opening must serve only to emphasize the enclosure of the whole.'

Right from the earliest planning stage, think how you will enjoy your secret space. I know what I want from the secret room at the bottom of my small city garden. I want peace, first of all, the kind of intensified stillness you find in medieval cloisters. I want to feel the seasons and the sun on my face, watch the haughty unfurling of leaves, catch the rhythms of the soil through my toes. Summer scents, gently falling water, an old but comfortable seat and plenty of natural greenery complete my

imagined idyll – imagined only because the pump for my small cascade has expired from overwork and the philadelphus I planted last spring has fallen prey to a particularly greedy colony of blackfly. Bugs thrive even in Eden (especially in Eden?).

There are other sorts of hidden rooms I could enjoy just as easily: a secret flower garden like the one at Blickling Hall, Norfolk, or Sir Geoffrey Jellicoe's free-form rose garden at Cliveden, Buckinghamshire. Best reached through the shady grove of evergreen oak (*Quercus ilex*) the rose garden opens in a glade like a head of petals (or a cabbage, for that matter). Jellicoe compared it to a painting by Paul Klee. In midsummer, a Kiftsgate rose clambers through surrounding trees; and archways sag with honeysuckle. Other hidden flower gardens I have seen bring the showy brightness of the herbaceous border to a woodland's cool green. Savoured in private, their enjoyment seems wilfully illicit.

And I have always longed for a walled garden. Since the Middle Ages, walled gardens in Europe have met a deep yearning for peace and protection, for keeping the outside world at bay. The sculptor Barbara Hepworth described finding her

Cornish studio at St Ives as 'a sort of magic'. For ten years she had passed by with her shopping bags, never suspecting that beyond the twenty-foot wall was a studio, a yard and a garden that retains its spell, even after her death. So does the walled Jardin des Colombières high above the bay at Menton in Provence, home of French surrealist Ferdinand Bac. Even walled fruit and vegetable gardens can include secret elements – seats and pools folded into alcoves, for example, or benches slid into niches, ringed with plants and ornamental herbs growing in pots. I like to sit with my back against a wall, hidden from view but not entirely; it makes me feel secure. A seat under a low, spreading apple tree or a flaming maple affords the same feeling of comfort.

Hadspen Garden in Somerset has a magnificent walled garden in the shape of a truncated oval. You enter through a decayed creeper-clad doorway into a riot of overspilling borders. But I like the walled corner of the potting shed garden best, because of its backwater calm and because it refuses to strive for effect. From the rickety seat you look over ferns and jungle-like vegetation to a three-sided wall that offers enclosure without crowding. This is a place to sit when the day's tasks are done.

Here, I think, in this image of quietness lies one of the secrets I am trying to uncover. Gardens become secret in the way they are used as well as in the way they are created. Where space is limited and you have room for only one hidden area, then almost inevitably this will become a place of retreat and point of contact with the natural world, however artificially contrived. I go to my secret garden when my spirits need revitalizing. Picasso has described this process in relation to painting. 'The painter,' he says, 'passes through states of fullness and of emptying. That is the whole secret of art. I take a walk in the forest of Fontainebleau. There I get an indigestion of greenness. I must empty this sensation into a picture.'

LEFT: A clipped Lawson cypress hedge (*Chamaecyparis lawsoniana* 'Allumii') shields a womb-like seating area, dark and secure and suitably private for the sharing of confidences.

RIGHT: Textured bark and humpy shrubs invite touching, creating interest close at hand.

FAR RIGHT: To plan a garden of hidden rooms, look first at how you organize the space. Trees, hedges, changes in level can all delineate separate areas. Here the semi-circular hedges are subtly varied in height and breadth.

A GARDEN OF MANY ROOMS

If a single secret area becomes a place of stillness, a garden of several rooms (or compartments, or cabinets) introduces the dynamic of movement. These gardens can be planned like stories with beginnings, middles, subplots, complications, and a satisfying end to make the enterprise worthwhile. They can even, like fiction, play around with post-modern tricks. 'Modern literary novelists,' says the writer David Lodge, 'wary of neat solutions and happy endings, have tended to invest their mysteries with an aura of ambiguity and to leave them unresolved.'

In organizing the narrative 'flow' through your garden, you will find there are only a limited number of ways in which your rooms can be fitted together. The most obvious progression is *linear*, with garden spaces arranged in sequence. Alternatively, you might want to *cluster* your rooms around an entry point, like petals at the end of a stalk. Or you can *stack* them one inside the other like Russian dolls and Chinese boxes. Smaller spaces are best clustered or stacked; linear progression, on the other hand, gives a sense of movement and discovery.

Chinese gardens offer inspiration to Western gardeners for their treatment of secret spaces, and especially the principles they embody. While many gardens in the West aspire to the

perfections of geometry, the Chinese tradition seeks to distil the essence of nature. Though their backdrops evoke the emptiness of bare silk on a calligrapher's scroll, Chinese gardens are nonetheless crammed with architecture: pavilions, bridges, paths, walls that define separate compartments. Secret spaces are especially encouraged – walls hidden by creepers, buildings partly concealed by trees, intimate places that allow you 'to gaze far away, as over endless waters' in an illusion of infinity. Inscriptions, chosen objects, and above all the names given to different pavilions, all add layers of meaning to the journey through these strange, manipulated landscapes, each 'cell' with its different purpose depending on the season and the time of day.

In a garden of many rooms, it is possible to plant and furnish each one in a separate style; larger American gardens often combine a huge variety of garden types. One fairly typical Californian garden at Montecito, for example, included a wild-flower field, brick-and-masonry gazebo with French Romanesque columns, knot garden, heliotrope garden, Spanish garden, Japanese garden, rock garden, orange and apricot orchards, and a small cactus garden. Gardens like these work best when each area has its own special focus within the overall

plan. The pallor of Vita Sackville-West's famous White Garden at Sissinghurst is a necessary antidote to the blazing oranges and yellows of the Cottage Garden, while her Nuttery becomes wilder when reached through the stiffly pleached Lime Walk.

But simply dividing a garden into rooms will not of itself create a sense of mystery. You must be much more cunning in your plans and vary the techniques of surprise and suspense. Advice about enclosures and entrances applies equally (only more so) to these larger gardens. Movement, in particular, opens the way for contrasts – between light and shade, or between different moods. A dark entrance, tunnelled through an ancient yew or twisted holly, inevitably stops the breath. The archway can be left wild and shaggy, or clipped, or marked with dark-painted trellis: the frisson in this case comes when 'nature' and 'control' collide. If the pathway veers to left or right (without obvious issue), so much the better. And when sunlight finally shines through, it turns leaves into silk – young leaves of copper beech especially.

In effecting the transition from one area to another, your principal tactics are surprise or suspense. Victorian Biddulph Grange celebrates the drama of surprise – walking through the garden is an exhilarating experience, for children just as much as for adults. A different approach – equally beguiling – is to tease expectations with partial views that open then are quickly denied. French philosopher Gaston Bachelard – a great dreamer of hidden corners who began his working life as a postman – has written eloquently about the daydreams provoked by doors. 'For the door is an entire cosmos of the Half-open,' he says in *The Poetics of Space*. 'In fact, it is one of its primal images, the very origin of a daydream that accumulates desires and temptations.'

Margery Fish's garden at East Lambrook Manor in Somerset shows how garden rooms can be 'secret' yet linked together with views and glimpses through the surrounding shrubbery. She bought the battered house and wilderness garden in 1937, looking especially for 'crooked paths and unexpected corners'.

Entering the garden by the old stone summerhouse, you are immediately faced with a choice of twisting paths – and choices demand that you become active rather than passive. As you weave your way around the garden, its most charming views are snatched glimpses of empty seats seen through 'frames' of green – a pair of oak nursery armchairs in Arts and Crafts style; and later, a simple wooden bench viewed across the top lawn. To be truly secret, these views would be denied, but then you wouldn't know they were there. A sudden view from the 'wrong' path makes the seats doubly tempting. And you still have to find your way through the shrubberies.

Paths carry special meaning for the secret gardener. At once functional and symbolic, they provide the essential elements of plot – linking, enticing, indicating the way forward (or back), teasing and comforting in equal measure. A path draws you

FAR LEFT: Brick archways that repeat themselves like baroque corridors – this is a classic architectural trick to draw you onwards.

CENTRE: Stone mask and subdued planting heighten the gloom of a walled folly cut with spyholes like a Chinese Garden.

LEFT: Sunken gardens are often delightfully unexpected – especially when unconventionally planted, as here.

OVERLEAF: Placing an urn off-centre is either annoying or intriguing, depending on your frame of mind.

onwards even if you don't know where you are going. To be part of the mystery, it, too, needs to be enclosed, to bend out of sight or to narrow into a vanishing point. A path that forks implies choice and hesitation. One that turns back on itself implies a change of heart. And by varying the texture and width, you can influence the speed at which your garden is traversed. Bricks laid lengthwise encourage people to hurry; those laid across the path invite you to pause. Wide paths suggest a stroll; narrow ones make you step faster. Cobbles are rarely trodden, while stepping stones introduce a note of caution. Gravel can be pressed and quick, or spongy like marshmallow.

Here are some favourite paths:

◊ The jungle boardwalk at Heligan, Cornwall, where it dips like a makeshift bridge over the ponds, snaking between giant gunnera, bamboos and tree ferns.

◊ A meadow path winding through the olive trees of the Roman *campagna* beyond Hadrian's villa at Tivoli, bright with poppies and wild flowers (but watch out for vipers, said the guide).

◊ A line of muddy grass between winter-bare beech hedges, tall as houses, at Bramham Park, Yorkshire, vanishing towards an enigmatic statue.

◊ Moss-covered steps disappearing into a rhododendron arch by the earthen mound at Rydal Mount in the English Lake District, just above the garden of my family home. (All summer long, the bushes echoed with the disembodied voices of Romantic tourists.)

Why do I like them so much, these paths that I see with my eyes shut? They make connections with my past, I suppose, though I have visited Bramham only once. The gamekeeper was in a fearful temper, we were told, and had let his dogs off the leash. (I can still hear their baying.) And all these paths transcend the functional with their invitation to take me *somewhere else*.

While your secret garden is still in your head (and ever after, as it takes shape on the ground), visit as many gardens as you can – public, private, the gardens of family and friends.

RIGHT: Tufts of spider plant and pure-white arum lilies (*Zantedeschia aethiopica*) lighten a sombre pool at the Palacio Viana, Cordoba, Spain, where a dreamy goddess pours perpetually from her jar.

FAR RIGHT: A stone monkey openly mocks the keepers of an Oxford garden, provoking eddies of unease.

The aim is not to 'steal' their ideas in executing neat copies of the original but rather to feed your own imagination. Whenever I write something new, I begin by reading voraciously – facts, mostly, but fiction too if I think it can prompt my own explorations. Plagiarism or homage? The division is sometimes dangerously close but I am reassured by the knowledge that the number of possible stories or plots is strictly limited. It's the telling that makes the difference.

Sometimes the gardens of others mean nothing at all; their 'secrets' seem contrived because they are not your secrets. Occasionally you visit one you could have planned and planted yourself. I found such a garden in an eastern suburb of Oxford. The solid wooden gateway to the street gave no hint of what lay beyond. It opened to a dark, gravelled, laburnum tunnel and a glimpse of Mediterranean architecture beyond, Oxford-hacienda style. Promising, so far, without touching me directly.

But I stepped into the garden with an uncanny sense of déjà-vu. Leading directly from the French windows was a plainish Italian *giardino segreto* set around a central octagonal flower bed hedged with knee-high box. A gap in the enclosing yew hedge opened to a stone and mosaic water feature, its flamboyant bird baths of dolphins and shells hinting at the magical cascade at the Palazzo Farnese, Caprarola, though still uncomfortably new. Among the many other areas to explore was a Sicilian courtyard for herbs, inspired by the cloisters of S. Giovanni Evangelista at Palermo; a shady bower where midsummer catkins of itea drip into a Romanesque bowl brimming with *Lamium* 'Hermann's Pride'; a grassy walk between columns of juniper where you feel that eyes in the shady undergrowth are watching you. (The eyes belong to a stone god, concealed in the cleft trunk of a holm oak.)

I left the most secret bit till last. Along the sunny side of the house, a grass path leads cheerfully towards the darkness at the far end. The foreground planting looks reassuringly familiar: flowering potentilla describing the shape of a Roman sarcophagus; dahlias; an Italian cypress; white foxgloves and hydrangeas; a miniature Weymouth pine which you pat as you pass. But as you near the end, and the path disappears out of sight, the planting becomes duller, more oppressive. Turn

the corner and you find yourself surrounded by stone figures that rear up out of the soil. A mocking stone monkey plays a squeeze box. Twisted holly and laurel create an uneasy twilight under the canopied shade of a weeping willow. One of the stone figures clasps both ears, its mouth open in a silent scream. Its message is confused. Ambiguity? Decay? The futility of human endeavour? The scream reminds me of the open mouth at Count Orsini's monster-inhabited estate at Bomarzo (described on page 128). Or the face of a screaming gargoyle from the ruined cascade at the Villa Aldobrandini, Frascati, I had once used on the cover of a fat thesis about 'spirit of place'. The epigram I chose came from Robert Harbison's *Eccentric Spaces*: 'Every garden is a replica, a representation, an attempt to recapture something ...'

A Garden of Green Rooms

Situated right on the busy Pacific coast, this Californian garden provides the setting for an utterly private drama of cool green spaces that slide into each other. This is theatre at its most direct, achieving intimacy and romance through simplicity of line rather than over-dressed frills. While each 'room' has its own intense focus, the transition from one to another has received equal thought.

Continuity has undoubtedly helped: created more than 80 years ago by Robert Chevalier, the garden is tended now by his daughter. An interior designer by trade, she has let the garden grow tall around her. 'So many people want to cut everything down to human scale,' she says of much current design. 'Nothing is allowed to grow over five or six feet high [1.5–2 metres] and shade is anathema. I prefer a shady dell, a long vista leading to a sunny meadow, variety, privacy and surprise.'

Surprise and suspense can be seen in the garden's use of gateways and paths that lead from one space to the next. Here you enter through a willow gate that tantalizes with its partial view of a pebbled path, rampantly planted with agapanthus, acanthus, bergenia, forget-me-not and watsonia. The gate is practical as well as decorative: it keeps out the deer who would otherwise devour everything. Descending into a small stream, the lily pond was built as a swimming pool in the 1920s. Now it creates a reflective heart to the garden, ringed with trees and tall shrubs that happily grow into each other. Along one edge, a low boxwood hedge draws the eye to another of the rooms.

The main pathway leads through a rose arbour planted with the blush-pink *Rosa* 'Cécile Brunner', giving no hint of the gardens on either side. The way ahead is blocked by a smother of vines. Turn sharp left and you find yourself on the Wedding Garden lawn, used as the name suggests for family festivities but also for more intimate occasions. The turf here is a fresh springy green: once the vegetable garden, natural grasses have been encouraged to grow in their place. High cypress walls shut out the world beyond, lending a distant air of the Moorish Generalife palace in Granada. The lower hedge of box defines a separate area of lawn beneath a fruiting apple. Another wall is formed, more informally, by hedge bamboo (the half-hardy *Bambusa glaucescens*). The garden has many other areas to explore: gardens for flowers, roses, rhododendrons, a sunken and a hillside garden, lawns and shrubberies. But these green rooms come closest to expressing the privacy, enclosure and mystery that make a garden truly secret.

ABOVE: A willow gate, kept shut against marauding deer, offers the first tempting view of the hidden lily pond. RIGHT: Encircled by evergreen shrubs and trees (pittosporum, *Choisya ternata*, holly and rhododendrons), the lily pond's calm is disturbed by wild mallards and an occasional heron.

VINE SCREEN

ROSE ARBOUR

WEDDING GARDEN

STEPS

HEDGE WITH TUNNELLED ARCHES

From the outer garden a gap in the rose arbour allows you to peek through to the Wedding Garden beyond.

The view down the Wedding Garden lawn is quietly formal, its lines broken by a bushy apple and another tunnelled gap in the cypress hedge.

6m/20ft

Edged with natural stone, informally laid, the pond's still waters mirror the tufted planting of ginger lilies, acanthus and ferns.

10

12

7

WILLOW GATE

13

11

14

WILLOW SEAT

14

LILY POND

15

14

17

STREAM

19

15

18

16

KEY TO PLANTING

1 Weeping cherry (*Prunus*)

2 Magnolia

3 Vine (*Muehlenbeckia complexa*)

4 Monterey cypress
(*Cupressus macrocarpa*)

5 *Rosa eglanteria*

6 *Rosa* 'Cécile Brunner'

7 Cotoneaster **8** Rhododendron

9 Acanthus

10 Flowering cherry (*Prunus*)

11 Holly (*Ilex aquifolium*)

12 Bird of Paradise shrub
(*Caesalpinia gilliesii*)

13 Pittosporum

14 Mexican orange blossom
(*Choisya ternata*)

15 Ginger lilies (*Hedychium*)

16 Ferns **17** Euonymus

18 Plum **19** Elaeagnus

20 Japanese crabapple
(*Malus floribunda*) **21** Box
(*Buxus microphylla* var. *japonica*)

22 *Juniperus × pfitzeriana*

23 *Crocosmia masoniorum*

24 *Solenopsis fluviatilis*

25 Bamboo (*Bambusa glaucescens*)

A dense hedge affords the comfort of enclosure while teasing the spirits with cutaway views into the next compartment.

ABOVE: Arbours and tunnels of clipped camellias are often found in old Portuguese gardens,
shining with flowers in early spring.

Intimate Retreats

Across a sunlit lawn, the doorway to a summerhouse
glistens in the shade. Quick, now – no one will
see you as you slip inside, lingering through the
long lazy afternoon, until shadows stretch into
evening and the air grows chill.

Dream spaces that exist out of place and out of time, the retreats of this chapter give the garden some of its strangest, most delightful hiding places. They are broadly of two kinds: garden buildings such as summerhouses, pavilions and gazebos; and 'living structures' – arbours, bowers, pergolas and tunnels – in which climbing plants or trees are trained to provide canopies and sometimes walls. However fantastical (or plain) from the outside, a summerhouse encloses you in a separate world that magnifies the pleasures of the senses: scent, sound, touch and sight. Who can fail to be seduced by its elusive temptations? Or do you seek rather to clothe yourself in a tangle of leaves, creating arbours or tunnels that twist out of sight, changing their dress with the seasons? Enticed into their cool greenery, you will find that opposites converge in subtle transformations: outside and inside, light into dark, nature into art.

RIGHT: The cast-iron bridge at the Swiss Garden, Bedfordshire, tempts you towards an improbably exotic Indian kiosk.

RIGHT: The summerhouse at Rydal Mount in Cumbria, William Wordsworth's final home, opens out to a majestic view of the lake. Built of vernacular stone and slate, the interior has rustic panelling and a cobbled floor.

TRADITION

The tradition for garden retreats (whether built or grown) naturally developed most strongly in harsh climates, in the countries surrounding the Mediterranean, for example, and throughout the Arab world. The earliest recorded arbours were the vine-laden pergolas of Ancient Egypt, seen on tomb decorations of the twelfth century BC. Arbours featured, too, in Ancient Rome, in the gardens of men like Pliny the Younger who lived in the first century AD. At his two villas near Rome and Tuscany, he married function to pleasure with a scattering of pavilions, towers, little temples, porticoes and covered walkways that brought nature and house together to make living out-of-doors extremely pleasurable.

As garden buildings were intended originally to provide relief from the climate, their main requirements were shade from the sun, open sides to attract the breezes, and proximity to water. The coolest paradise gardens of Islam had a pavilion at their heart, often placed above the intersection of the four water channels that formed the traditional design, symbolizing the four rivers of life. Here, the earthly paradise appealed to the senses and to the spirit:

> '*On couches with linings of brocade shall they recline* [promises the Koran to the faithful] *and the fruit of the two gardens shall be within easy reach: Therein shall be damsels with retiring glances, whom neither man nor djinn hath touched: Like jacinths and pearls ...*'

But pavilions and garden retreats were not restricted to Islam. Ideas and designs crossed continents and cultures, inspiring an eclecticism that continues to this day. Whether erected as hunting

stands or banqueting houses, for eating desserts and light confections or for fleeting *amours*, these buildings were dedicated to pleasure in architectural styles to match: delicate, architectural *capricci*, constructed of materials that could not last, alas, but contemporary descriptions and pattern books give some idea of the fantasies they inspired. Thomas Wright's *Universal Architecture* of 1755 offered six original designs for arbours. Exquisitely etched against a backdrop of gnarled rocks and fluffy trees, these included arbours 'of the Cave or Cabin Kind', 'of the Hut or Hovel-kind' and 'of the Parasol Kind', as well as an aviary, a druid's hut and an arbour for outdoor entertainments.

Throughout their history, some garden retreats have celebrated solitude: places of escape for scholars, hermits, poets, gentlefolk and all those weary of the world. You can still visit the stone summerhouse built in the late 1660s by Sir Daniel Fleming of Rydal Hall, in the English Lake District, overlooking the lower waterfall on his estate. Here, he retired from the pressures of life and his thirteen children. Across the way is Rydal Mount, where William Wordsworth lived his last four decades, composing poems as he paced the top terrace and sometimes in his rustic summerhouse at the highest point of the garden, where the view swoops suddenly down to encompass the shining lake below.

Sir Daniel's retreat bears witness to the sound advice of his contemporary, writer and gentleman John Woolridge. In his book of 1677, *Systema Horti-Culturae or The Art of Gardening*, Woolridge declared that the crowning pleasure of a garden was 'a place of repose, where neither Wind, Rain, Heat, nor Cold

RIGHT: This thatched tea-house is marooned on an island in Tatton Park's Japanese garden in Cheshire, created in 1910 around a darkly secret pool.

CENTRE: Charles Hamilton dotted his park at Painshill, Surrey, with eighteenth-century conceits: this wooden Gothic temple is painted to resemble stone.

FAR RIGHT: The Red House at Painswick in Gloucestershire (photographed before its final red wash) is reached by converging paths from either side that conceal its asymmetrical design.

can annoy you. This small Edifice, usually term'd a Pleasure-house or Banquetting-house, may be made at some remote Angle of your Garden: For the more remote it is from your House, the more private will you be from the frequent disturbances of your Family or Acquaintances ...'

And what of the bowers and pavilions created especially for seduction? Nothing remains of Rosamund's fabled bower, at Woodstock. The Chinese pavilions set aside for imperial concubines are empty now. And the majority of guidebooks to follies like Sir Francis Dashwood's Temple of Venus at West Wycombe, Buckinghamshire, remain coyly silent on their explicitly erotic metaphor. (Dashwood was a leading member of the orgiastic Hell-Fire Club of the eighteenth century.) Love goes underground, it seems, although the imagination lingers.

Garden history returns us to more certain ground when we look at the way fashions for different kinds of retreat changed across the ages. By 1625, when Francis Bacon wrote his celebrated treatise *Of Gardens*, covered 'alleys' or tunnelled arbours and 'stately arched hedges' had become a regular feature of the garden, hung with birdcages and spheres of coloured glass to catch the sun. Though not especially 'secret', these alleys were intended to give shade and privacy to those walking in the gardens.

The royal palace at Het Loo in the Netherlands – laid out for William and Mary in the late seventeenth century – contains a magnificently restored network of arboured pathways in the Queen's private gardens. Looking from the outside like a green arcade pierced with windows and decorated with tented hats at each end, the inside is refreshingly intimate, a relief from the open splendour of the 'public' gardens beyond. Your feet scrape the gravel as you stroll beneath the solid, vaulted frame, crafted in wood and supporting immaculately trained hornbeam, pausing to admire the framed views of clipped hedges and potted exotics – orange trees, bottlebrushes, spiky palms and phormiums.

By the mid-eighteenth century, however, tastes had veered away from galleried walks like these to a more 'natural' landscape dotted with small buildings. Such buildings had a dual function: as focal points in the view and as retreats or resting places on a walk around the estate. Tastes were decidedly eclectic. Turkish tents appeared on the sandy wastes of Surrey at Painshill; Egyptian pyramids in the eerily fantastic Désert de Retz on the outskirts of Paris and in Yorkshire at Castle Howard; rustic root-houses in genteel Badminton, Avon (to a design by Thomas Wright); Chinese pagodas and tea-houses just about everywhere in the style dubbed 'anglo-chinois'.

One garden bursting with eighteenth-century whimsy is Painswick Rococo Garden in Gloucestershire, recently restored to original views painted by Thomas Robins the Elder. Architectural styles embrace the Red House in asymmetrical gothic; a Doric seat with rustic porticoes; Gothic alcove; a tunnelled arbour planted with laburnum, honeysuckle, jasmine and clematis; and the crenellated 'Eagle House' sunk into the hillside with a squashed hexagonal top. Though winding paths make some attempt at concealment, these buildings were designed to be both seen and enjoyed as stages on a journey round the garden (it is not very large).

Throughout the nineteenth century, the summerhouse flourished as a poetic (often sentimental) conceit, hidden in 'enchanted dells' beside 'gushing rills'. The taste for melancholy gothic spread as far as Victorian California; in one estate, known as Lachryma Montis (Tear of the Mountain), the owners built a gothic summerhouse at the edge of a lawn, beside a cast-iron fountain. With the turn of the century came a new emphasis on good, solid design and a return to fashion of well-crafted pergolas and arbours. Lutyens and Jekyll in England, and Frederick Law Olmsted and Beatrix Farrand in America all produced fine examples that survive to this day.

SUMMERHOUSES AND PAVILIONS

Although the names of garden buildings are often used interchangeably, a summerhouse usually refers to a lightweight building in a garden or park, intended to provide shade in summer ('shadow-house' was an earlier name). Garden pavilions are even lighter in construction, open-sided like the bandstands of an English park or the viewing pavilions that dot the gardens and landscapes of China.

> *'Meditating thus I arrived at a high, rusty iron gate. Through the railings I could see an avenue bordered with poplar trees and also a kind of summer house or pavilion. Two things dawned on me at once, the first trivial and the second almost incredible: the music came from the pavilion and that music was Chinese.'*
> JORGE LUIS BORGES, *FICCIONES*

The choices you face when planning a secret retreat are inevitably bound up together: choice of site, of structure, and of planting. But first, consider what your retreat is *for*. Are you solitary or convivial by nature? Which matters most, peace or entertainment? Do you long to shut yourself away entirely, or do you wish rather to create a quiet corner for meetings with friends?

Site is the next consideration. In the smallest gardens, where you cannot hope to hide your summerhouse from the main house, you will have little option but to treat it as a focal point from the outside and to use planting to increase feelings of privacy within. Whether your building is square, round, hexagonal, octagonal, or any other shape, it will usually have just a single entrance. This should be angled to give the longest view across the garden (usually the diagonal), and to shut out as far as possible your view of the house. It may also be possible to 'borrow' views beyond the garden wall – other people's trees, for example, a church spire or distant hills. Even encircling buildings can be coaxed into providing a cocoon, softened by your own planting. In such surroundings, an open pavilion would almost certainly feel too exposed.

How to enhance the privacy of your summerhouse through planting is very much a question of taste. If the structure has trellised sides, climbers are an obvious choice: roses such as

LEFT: Hidden deep in a German garden, an open pavilion stands like an enigmatic bus shelter at the woodland's edge – a perfect retreat from which to enjoy its rustling wildlife and fidgety light.

RIGHT: The New Zealand sub-jungle provides a natural setting to hide this simple hut, which acts as both a look-out and retreat.

FAR RIGHT: Popular since the eighteenth century, rustic huts still exert a primitive appeal.

OVERLEAF LEFT: A strangely ornate summerhouse hidden in a forest recalls the wood-cutter's cottage of folk tales.

OVERLEAF CENTRE: Open structures offer a privileged viewpoint, both cocooning the viewer and framing the view.

OVERLEAF RIGHT: Sound construction and good, solid materials are here softened by climbing roses and thrusting kiwi fruit.

Rosa mulliganii, *R.* 'Mme Alfred Carrière', or the exquisitely formed light-pink flowers of *R.* 'Climbing Cécile Brunner'; scented climbers like summer jasmine (*Jasminum officinale*, or the pink-tinged *J. officinale* f. *affine*) and honeysuckle. (*Lonicera japonica* 'Halliana' is both vigorous and dependable; for richer colours try the trumpet honeysuckle, *L. sempervirens*, with its scarlet-orange tubular flowers, or the wine-red of *L. periclymenum* 'Serotina'.) Good flowering evergreen climbers include star jasmine, *Trachelospermum jasminoides*, with its sworls of pure white, and *Pileostegia viburnoides*, fluffed cream in late summer, which is slow-growing but excellent for shady aspects. Among the many clematis varieties on offer, consider some of the smaller-flowered types whose delicacy can be best appreciated close at hand: the evergreen *Clematis armandii*, early-flowering cultivars of *C. alpina* such as 'Frankie' (pale blue) or 'Willy' (pale pink), or the vigorous late-flowering *C.* × *fargesioides* 'Paul Farges'. If speed of growth is a priority, vines and hops will quickly bury your hiding place, while the

Russian vine (now renamed *Fallopia baldschuanica*) will turn it into a mop within a mere couple of seasons, frothed white with late-summer flowers.

Larger gardens naturally give you more choice of site. You may want to hide your summerhouse completely, banishing it towards the boundaries and giving only fleeting glimpses to anyone venturing into the garden. You can achieve this partly by the way you direct your paths or 'routes' through the garden, and partly by the use of screening shrubs and trees. If your aim is to block all sight of the summerhouse, you will want to plant dense, bushy shrubs: bamboos, viburnums, choisya, ceanothus, enkianthus, rhododendrons, berberis, banks of roses or thorns or the dripping silk-tassel bush (*Garrya elliptica* 'Evie' produces especially long catkins, up to 30 centimetres or 12 inches). You could also introduce evergreens like yew, but beware of creating gloom by association. (Laurel always makes me think of Victorian shrubberies; and yew was planted in the eighteenth century expressly to evoke a melancholy mood.) If your aim is more to tantalize than conceal, opt for shrubs and trees with a lighter touch: a pinkish gauze of tamarisk (*Tamarix tetrandra* or *T. ramosissima*); the feathery leaves of golden elder (*Sambucus racemosa* 'Plumosa Aurea'); spiky bristles of the Australian bottlebrush (*Callistemon citrinus*); twisted stems of corkscrew hazel (*Corylus avellana* 'Contorta'); or thickets of rustling quicksilver (*Elaeagnus* 'Quicksilver'). Surround your summerhouse with purple-leaved smoke bushes (*Cotinus coggygria* 'Royal Purple') and it will appear to float away in a summer haze of pink inflorescence.

If you have lots of space to play with – or if you are working with a very constrained site – you may want to use the summerhouse as a point of transition between one area and the next – much as Victorian James Bateman used the Cheshire Cottage at Biddulph Grange to lead the unsuspecting visitor from the Pinetum into Egypt. A summerhouse or pavilion placed at the elbow of an L-shaped garden can work in just the same way, as the gateway into a hidden area. For the surprise to work, you may need to add side screens that block views into the secret garden, or *trompe-l'oeil* devices that confuse our perceptions of space and geometry.

Open pavilions, by their nature, will rarely work as hiding places. Their role is largely aesthetic: to define the space in which they stand, framing the view and concentrating your enjoyment. If you want to incorporate one into a secret garden, it is best to plan the garden so that you come upon it by chance – at the edges of a wood, for example, or like the pavilion I saw at Het Loo, which appeared to levitate above a sea of ox-eye daisies.

Climate will obviously influence your choice of structure, especially extremes of sun, wind or rain. Sloping roofs are most appropriate for rain, and semi-permeable windbreaks needed for regions with strong prevailing winds. Sunlight is best slatted through fine laths of bamboo or filtered through canopied climbers and vines. Remember, too, to orientate your summerhouse so that it catches the sun you most want, whether morning or evening. Or opt for a grander and more expensive version pivoted on a revolving base that you can turn to meet (or flee) the sun.

As for the structure itself, the usual advice is that its architecture should reflect the style of the main house, to prevent constant argument. In *The Education of a Gardener*, for example, English designer Russell Page declared that only in isolated sites would he permit himself the extravagance of a folly, 'an exotic garden structure or ornament made to point or accentuate a deliberately "escapist" garden.' But secret gardens *are* places of escape; and designers have always produced some of their most imaginative work for lightweight garden buildings

that are not meant to last forever. So providing your summerhouse or pavilion can sit contentedly in its own space, your choice is limited only by taste and pocket: rustic thatch, modern stone and steel, Californian pool-house, Mexican adobe, Greek temple, Turkish tent, Chinese tea-house, Mogul pavilion or a style that is outrageously its own. Most garden shows and the larger garden centres offer a wide range of models you can buy off-the-shelf and then adapt to your own taste. A neighbour of mine in an ordinary north London street has, over the years, built himself a folly of a summerhouse that started life as a simple shed, veered towards Indian Gothic, then metamorphosed into a rustic railway station, still with a touch of the Orient.

The summerhouses I want most are not yet built. The first is a place in which to write: small and very plain, like a sentry box with a seat, a table and a decent view. It should have the resiny smell of newly hewn wood.

My second is a place of easy companionship: a wooden hexagon, open at the front and cut with lattice windows on the other five sides. The wood is dark-stained to aid concealment. Small and encircling, the interior fills with restless green light that turns gold in the evening. Placed out of sight of the house, it turns to face the path as I don't want to be caught unawares.

Planting is wild but not neglected: old scented roses, the blushest pink or pure white (like the violet-scented *Rosa banksiae*, which grows so profusely in California); honeysuckle; spice-scented wintersweet (*Chimonanthus praecox*) to savour in winter.

If I lived by the sea, I might try to evoke the wild loneliness of the dunes with a beachcomber's hut hidden by grasses: stripy spires of *Miscanthus sinensis* 'Variegatus', its leaves banded with creamy white and green, or the even taller *Stipa gigantea*, planted to catch the sun through its golden filaments.

When your summerhouse is finally built, pay attention to the small touches that will add to its enjoyment. Will you need tables and chairs for eating and drinking out-of-doors? What about a small chest for things often left behind – a bottle-opener, for example, and a book? Do you want candles or storm lanterns or lighting of a more permanent kind? Think, too, about the objects or ornaments that can help to reinforce the atmosphere you want to create: old pots or stones, for example, or a sculpted garden god. Venetian gardens in particular are filled with mysterious objects haphazardly collected and then apparently abandoned – stone carvings, amphorae, languid maidens and discarded angels. Look after your space, too. Dirt and obvious neglect are atmospheric in small measure only.

RIGHT: Pavilions and gazebos act as both focal points and private retreats. Rich red roses and fluffy smoke bush sweep the eye along the path towards the copper-domed pavilion of Mogul inspiration.

FAR RIGHT: Without its birdcage gazebo, this quiet yellow-and-white corner would look almost unkempt; shelter and seat give meaning and life to its casual planting (*Alchemilla mollis*, white roses and campanulas, false acacia).

GAZEBOS

Gazebos, by definition, are designed to give views out across the garden or its surroundings. (The word comes from joke-Latin: 'I gaze'. In Spain they are called *miradors*; in France, *gloriettes*; and *belvederes* in Italy.) Their elevated position makes them hard to conceal from view, unless they are pushed right to the boundary, although you can disguise the paths that reach them. Sunken hedgerows or tunnels roofed with coppiced willow, climbers and espaliered fruit can be made to snake around their base. Or you can hide the 'entrance' at the back, making a puzzle out of how to gain entry. A raised maze I visited in a Dutch garden felt intensely private although the hedge reached only chest height and you were visible from all around.

The gazebos I like best are constructed from delicate materials like wire, or American designer Thomas Church's elegantly latticed designs with peaked hats in slatted wood. I also like gazebos built in vernacular materials that root them into their surroundings. In *Arts and Crafts Gardens*, Gertrude Jekyll described her own gazebo at Munstead Wood, Surrey: a little house reached by a winding flight of steps, 'most often used when there is thunder about, for watching the progress of the storm'. In the accompanying photograph, one of the four side openings is weather-boarded shut to prevent views of a neighbour's house and garden – an admirable courtesy.

A gazebo is especially welcome in an enclosed garden because it releases the tensions of claustrophobia. One built at Sissinghurst in memory of Sir Harold Nicolson gives splendid views from the far corner of the orchard into the Kentish Weald. The Swiss Garden in Bedfordshire, by contrast, though of roughly similar size, concentrates all its views inwards, even from the two-storey thatched Swiss Chalet at its heart. This can, at times, feel oppressive. For a secret gazebo at the boundary, site the structure on a mound concealed by trees and shrubs. The view out then becomes the surprise.

ARBOURS, PERGOLAS, TUNNELS AND BOWERS

The definitions for these and other similar structures very quickly run into each other, like circular paths. The term 'pergola' comes from Italian and is usually used to describe a covered walk formed of climbing plants or fruit trees trained over a structure of uprights and connecting joists or arches. When the structure or its canopy becomes especially dense, it shades into a 'tunnel-arbour', known in old English as a 'herber' and in French as an *allée en berceau*. The terms 'arbour' and 'bower' are often used interchangeably. I take an 'arbour' in its dictionary sense as 'a shady retreat enclosed by trees or climbing plants', often shaped as a curving arch but sometimes elongated into a short tunnel. The word 'bower' is also used to describe a leafy shelter, although it is usually smaller than an arbour and may be formed simply by trained or over-hanging trees. The element common to all these features is a living canopy of climbing plants or trees, either shaped over an open framework or trained to do the job on its own.

In her first book, *Wood and Garden* (1899), Gertrude Jekyll perfectly described the sensation of entering the cool depths of a pergola in summer: 'It feels wonderfully dark at first, this gallery of cool greenery, passing into it with one's eyes full of light and colour, and the open-sided summer-house at the end looks like a black cavern; but on going into it, and sitting down on one of its broad, low benches, one finds that it is a pleasant, subdued light, just right to read by.'

Though pergolas are open structures, they can be made to feel very private by swags of planting dripping from the cross-beams or by playing around with the levels. The structure must always be strong enough to bear the considerable weight, and high enough to give sufficient head room beneath the cascading greenery. Pergolas that are sunk 50 centimetres (1½ feet) or more below the level of the surrounding garden also feel deliciously secret, as do ones that curve out of view. Pergolas in North American gardens – like their Latin or Spanish models – are often used to provide the transition between the shade of the house and the full sunlight of the garden beyond. These, too, are 'secret' in feel rather than reality and because of the partial shade – and partial views – they introduce.

A grand example to emulate can be found in The Hill Garden near Hampstead Heath, designed by Thomas Mawson for Lord Leverhulme and begun in 1905. For years one of London's secret gardens, romantic in its creeping decay, the pergola walk was restored in the 1990s, regaining its grace and beauty and losing only a little of its mystery. I like it best towards sunset, when the raised pergola slips into shadow and figures appear and disappear behind the double rows of pillars on either side. Planting is suitably lush: the twining *Schisandra rubriflora* and the glossier evergreen *Trachelospermum asiaticum*, its fragrant creamy white flowers turning yellow with age; rampant kiwi fruit (*Actinidia deliciosa*); the shrubby *Colquhounia coccinea* and *Carpenteria californica*; climbing and rambling roses by the score.

Gertrude Jekyll in fact advised against roses for pergolas, claiming that they soon ran leggy and only flowered at the top, out of sight. Instead she favoured vines, jasmine, Virginia creeper, the weirdly-flowered aristolochia, and everyone's favourite, wisteria. I particularly like the slightly waxy, white-veined leaves of Chinese Virginia creeper (*Parthenocissus henryana*) and blue-flowered forms of passion flower, such as *Passiflora caerulea*.

Tunnel-arbours are essentially linking devices that lead from one area of the garden to the next. Their 'drama' is that of surprise and manipulation, opening into sudden views and tightly controlling your progression through light and shade. As well as helping to create a good bone structure for your garden – with strong verticals and mass – they contribute to its itinerary and are best used to heighten suspense. You can do this either by placing a highly charged object at the vanishing point – a sculpture or carving, for example, or an ornamental pot; or by turning a corner and leaving only the sketchiest hint of the tunnel's destination.

Hornbeam, twisted holly and rhododendrons all make mysterious tunnels (the red trunks of old rhododendron especially), although you will need to wait a decade or more to achieve the density you want. Plant young specimens at hedging distance, generally between 45 and 60 centimetres apart (18 inches to 2 feet), and train them over ironwork arches or rustic larch or fir poles that can later be allowed to decay. You could also try beech, which keeps a coat of dead leaves through the winter; or for a lighter mood, try cordoned fruit trees, golden hop, roses, white scented jasmine and the honeysuckles and wild vines so beloved by Francis Bacon and his Elizabethan contemporaries.

'Living' tunnel-arbours grown from coppiced willow rods can be very satisfying. I saw one in Hampshire that was to be used as a skittle alley. Planted in winter from freshly cut stems – stuck 30 centimetres (1 foot) deep in the earth and 15–20 centimetres (6–8 inches) apart – the owner described its sprouting as positively biblical. Another tunnel in Kent was slightly sunken and planted like a hedgerow with suckers and seedlings from around the garden: cornus and laburnum, dog roses and wild hop.

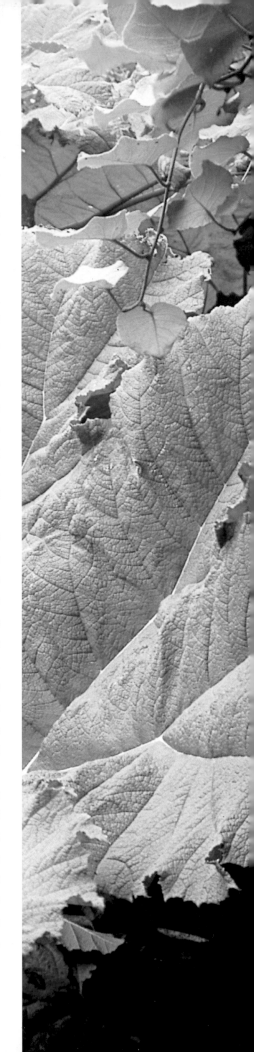

RIGHT: This criss-cross wire frame, romantically planted, satisfies most of the senses at a single sitting: scented honeysuckle (*Lonicera japonica*), tactile cobbled floor, summer shading, and a speckling of bright coloured roses and *Clematis integrifolia*.

FAR RIGHT: Secret gardens need quiet corners for reading and sitting, where their essence is best enjoyed.

If pergolas and tunnels are designed for movement, bowers and arbours provide the quiet, enclosed corners for private conversations and solitary musings. These I would tuck well out of view: cradled by hedges, in the folds of borders, backed against a wall, in the furthest reaches of the garden.

As a model for my secret arbour I might choose the rustic poles and wisteria camped (a little forlornly) in meadow grass at Nymans, Sussex, within the walled garden. When I saw it last, it looked dangerously close to collapse, and I wanted to give it a happier setting. But stepping between the rickety poles was like entering another world, a world of writhing stems and translucent blossom shivering like specks of opal, a world of drama and light-beyond-the-darkness. Laburnum tunnels leave me sated. This left me longing for more. And so I visited the rest of the garden on a leash, returning often to the arbour's strange quiet. The notes I wrote that day are maddeningly sparse: 'Twisted liana stems. Freckle of blossom. Bees. Bluebells and dead daffodils.'

You can buy arbour frames in all manner of materials: wood, metal, plastic-coated steel, wrought-iron. Frames can be planted or left plain like an artist's sketch, requiring a leap of the imagination to complete the leafy enclosure. Trellis, like ironwork, defines space without enclosing it. Consult as many pattern books as you can – new ones and old. These features are relatively easy to construct yourself (or to get made for you on site). Ones that meet your own fantasies will almost always work better than those bought off-the-shelf.

Any small weeping tree can be clipped and trained to give you a bower that needs only a seat, and a small table, to create a secret den. Trees to choose include: weeping pear (*Pyrus salicifolia* 'Pendula'); mulberry (*Morus alba* 'Pendula'); silver birch (the dome-shaped *Betula pendula* 'Youngii' or the even more drooping *B. pendula* 'Laciniata'); beech (*Fagus sylvatica* 'Purpurea Pendula' has blackly purple leaves and a height and spread of 3 metres or 9 feet); or weeping versions of larger trees such as ash (*Fraxinus excelsior* 'Pendula'), lime (especially *Tilia* 'Petiolaris'), and willow (*Salix babylonica* or *S.* × *sepulcralis* var. *chrysocoma*). A tiny weeping willow is *S. caprea* 'Kilmarnock' (growing to only 1.5 to 2 metres – 5 to 6 feet – depending on grafting height).

Tunnels, arbours and bowers linger in the memory. Here are some special favourites:

◊ For resting on a walk: the early Georgian bus-shelter seats by William Kent at Rousham, Oxfordshire, painted a cool green and hiding under trees by the bowling-green terrace.

◊ For evening drinks by a wildlife pool: a hexagonal arbour of poles roofed with Bacchanalian vines and hop, the point of the 'roof' an upside-down chandelier in wrought-iron.

◊ For tea and views: a leafy bower shaped like a tea-cosy at the edge of a terrace, made from three small weeping pear trees tied together over a metal arch and encouraged to knit into a single mass.

◊ For private conversations: a curving stone bench supported by lions set in an upturned 'soap dish' made of a trellised wood and hung with climbers: passion flower and clematis (the evergreen *Clematis armandii* and early-flowering *C. cirrhosa* var. *balearica*, and the blue, bell-shaped *C. alpina*).

◊ For strolling down a sun-baked hillside: the hooped trellis tunnels at Linderhof in Bavaria, supporting a roof of hornbeam and lime that filters the light to a watery green.

◊ For fugitive meetings with a friend: I shan't tell, except to say that this bower is guarded by a pair of stone sphinxes with sly smiles and reached by a gravel path that gives early warning of another's approach.

A Garden of Many Retreats

A hillside site overlooking farmland, a love of secret corners and the artist-owners' skill at giving the imagination concrete form have created a garden whose surprises change and multiply with the seasons. Twenty years ago or more, the 'garden' consisted of a brambly hill and a flattened area of rose beds and a glasshouse attached to the curving stable block of a large country house. Over the years, the owners have patiently imposed a natural order on their cultivated ground, matching the shapes and rhythms of their garden to the fields and hedgerows below.

The former rose garden was transformed first, into a grid-shaped paradise garden of intimately hedged spaces with plants (rather than water) at its heart. A vine-covered pergola squeezes between a sumach and an *Acer palmatum* 'Sango-kaku'. Towards the side runs a tunnel-arbour of espaliered apple. Both give the garden height and mass, inviting you to step inside. The lower terrace (a riotous vegetable garden) is more open in character: a grapevine tunnel and a birdcage pavilion of welded steel sketch the idea of enclosure, without shielding you from view.

The best hiding places can be found in the woodland garden that wraps itself around the curving wall of the house. Paths lead up and down to secret spaces: a seat with valley view beneath shining maples; a stone bench swirling into the overhang of a rhododendron; a turf hut built to give the children a taste of Iron-age living; a mock-Tudor butcher's stall abandoned in a thicket; an open metal gazebo in the shape of Cinderella's coach, made from the protective casing of transatlantic cable wire – base metal transmuted into fairy tale.

Ask the owners which retreat they like best and they will say it depends on the season and the time of day. The moods evoked are subtly different, too. Some are best enjoyed in company, others are designed for solitary reading or simply admiring the view. All slip sympathetically into the landscape so that you can come upon them by surprise, and all can be enjoyed by adults and children alike.

Just as gardens grow and decay, so new structures are always springing to life. The latest is a Chinese summerhouse painted a startling deep plum red and set on the bottom lawn next to a fine *Acer griseum*. Again the site has been carefully chosen. With the house at your back, you look across to the end of the tunnel-arbour and the over-spilling paradise garden towards the open country beyond: to the pleasures of intimacy is added the expansiveness of space.

ABOVE: The fronds of a weeping mulberry (*Morus alba* 'Pendula') hang like a bead curtain before the small pond. RIGHT: The turf hut has been stoutly constructed from salvaged materials, its roof covered with thick polythene and compost. Spring bulbs give way to summer poppies and daisies.

Hidden among
the ornamental
thistles (*Onopordum
nervosum*), fennel
and poppy heads
of the vegetable
garden, a rickety
wooden seat offers
an unexpected
hiding place.

A tunnel-arbour
of apple borders
one edge of the
paradise garden,
drawing you towards
the greenhouse
and terrace as
it envelops you in
bright, fresh green.

LOWER GARDEN

CONSERVATORY   9   10

1

CHINESE
SUMMERHOUSE

2

8

POND

PERGOLA

APPLE TUNNEL

5

4

7

6

22

3

23

GREENHOUSE

24   24

VEGETABLE GARDEN

SEAT   PAVILION

25

VINE ARCH

At the highest point of the garden stands an elegant gazebo fashioned from reclaimed transatlantic cable wire.

GAZEBO

STONE SEAT

FALLEN CHESTNUT TREE

PATH UNDER TREE

STEPS

BRIDGE

UPPER GARDEN

ICE HOUSE

TERRACE

TURF HUT

KEY TO PLANTING

1 *Sorbus cashmiriana*
2 *Acer griseum*
3 Pear (*Pyrus salicifolia*)
4 Sumach (*Rhus typhina*)
5 *Cotinus coggygria*
Purpureus Group
6 *Acer palmatum* 'Sango-kaku'
7 *Corylus avellana* 'Contorta'
8 *Morus alba* 'Pendula' **9** *Mahonia*
10 Holly (*Ilex aquifolium*)
11 *Symphoricarpos* **12** Bamboo
13 Rhododendron **14** Birch
(*Betula pendula*) **15** Beech
(*Fagus sylvatica*) **16** *Sorbus*
'Joseph Rock' **17** *Prunus* 'Ukon'
18 Fragrant snowbell (*Styrax
obassia*) **19** Lime (*Tilia*)
20 Fig (*Ficus*) **21** Pampas grass
(*Cortaderia selloana*)
22 *Choisya ternata* **23** White
lilac (*Syringa*) **24** Fan-trained
fruit trees **25** Giant thistle
(*Onopordum nervosum*)

Tendrils of hop (*Humulus lupulus*) curl alluringly across the pavilion's open roof without obscuring the sky.

9m/30ft

ABOVE: This tiny city garden combines foliage interest with a swirl of blue-brick paving around a shady apple tree.

Urban Oases

Traffic noise dims into insignificance as

you step through a curtain into hallowed space,

cool and sheltered, luxuriantly green.

Your world is shrinking to the sensual pleasures

of this walled enclosure; heaven in a shoebox.

Paradise begins with a garden, its elements simple and timeless: enclosure, stillness, water and ornament, planting that shrugs its wildness into our ordered lives. Green and fragrant, shimmered by fountains or dark reflecting pools, the urban oasis meets our deepest need: to be shielded from the constant stresses and obligations of the clamouring world outside. But the small enclosed courtyard is not the only refuge in a city. Rooftops, too, offer city dwellers the chance of flight from earth-bound chores towards a place where you can see without being seen. Here, above the noise and fumes of the city, the excitement of 'prospect' collides with the comfort of 'refuge' in a merging of buildings and sky. Burrow or nest, walled enclosure or rooftop eyrie, these are landscapes whose enjoyment goes beyond aesthetics and design to touch a common core of human experience – survival in a harsh and often hostile environment.

RIGHT: A Mediterranean courtyard brings a lushly green image of
Eden to the centre of the house, viewed and enjoyed from shaded arcades.

TRADITION

Courtyard gardens borrow from traditions that hark back to our earliest civilizations. Whole cities have grown up with narrow streets that give no hint of the walled paradises within: cities like Suzhou in China and Isfahan in Iran. Inevitably the tradition of secrecy grows strongest where the pressure on space is most intense: Venice is a prime example. 'In no other city,' wrote Cristiana Moldi-Ravenna and Tudy Sammartini in *Secret Gardens in Venice*, 'is the garden such an element of complicity, an excuse to arrive at one's goal via winding roads, alluding to a world that can only be intuited but never grasped.'

Serenity is the mood generally associated with the most inspiring courtyards of all – the courtyard gardens of Islam that offer a necessary escape from the desert's blistering skies.

Throughout the Muslim world, whether found in mosques or theological colleges, in bazaars, inns or private homes, courtyard gardens share a common purpose and identity that is both practical and spiritual. To their gifts of light and cool air, delivered into the very heart of the house, they add intimations of paradise and of the inner life of the individual.

'The Persian conceived his garden as a small and fertile oasis set in a huge barren landscape,' said Sir Geoffrey Jellicoe to a convention of landscape architects in Vienna. 'It was a kind of sanctuary, and its name, Paradise (a walled enclosure), soon came to acquire a wider association.' Abstract geometry, richly textured surfaces and the refreshment of water and shade created the perfect place for quiet contemplation – a mood that finds its echo in the frantic world of today.

Japan offers another ancient model that points to the same concentration of energy in confined spaces. Most Japanese courtyards have been influenced by the tea-garden that developed from the sixteenth century as a setting for the highly ritualized tea ceremony and its elegant discussion of philosophy and art. To sustain the proper atmosphere, two sorts of garden were required: the mood-inducing *roji* or 'dewy path' leading up to the tea-house; and the sober *tsuboniwa* or enclosed garden that was viewed from the tea-room itself. Together they gave the impression of a rustic hideaway that had been buried deep within the forest.

The setting for a tea-garden was restrained: moss, ferns, a handful of well-behaved shrubs and evergreens like azaleas pruned into boulders. Three features became indispensable: a stepping-stone path to reach the house, a stone lantern to light the way, and a stone water basin to wash away impurities. Function and aesthetics went hand-in-hand: the garden's tranquillity and seclusion were enhanced by shadowy lantern light, and any feelings of claustrophobia dispelled by limpid reflections in the water of the stone basin.

China, too, has a tradition of courtyard design that continues to inspire today. As the chapter on hidden rooms suggested, whole gardens were conceived as a series of interlocking courtyards to give an impression of infinity, each element chosen for its wider resonances. For Ji Cheng, author of the seventeenth-century treatise on garden-making *Yuan Yi*, gardening was based on illusion, its aim to capture the 'life spirit' of a place and of nature – even in the heart of a city.

Enclosed gardens in the Christian West can also lay claim to symbolic origins. Medieval Europe offers the model of the *Hortus Conclusus* or secret garden-within-a-garden, its symbolism reaching back to the Song of Solomon and the cult of the Virgin Mary: 'A garden inclosed is my sister, my spouse; a spring shut up, a fountain sealed …' Besides the kitchen and physic gardens,

many buildings in the Middle Ages had small enclosed pleasure gardens: the 'flowery mead' that appears in later illustrations, bordered with red and white roses, madonna lilies, peony, flag iris and bulbs, the trellis walls hung with honeysuckle and roses. These early gardens were small and simple, with raised turf seats, perhaps a fountain and an arbour. 'Men longed for peace after the centuries of war,' wrote Nan Fairbrother in her eloquent *Men and Gardens*, 'and in a harsh world a garden was a secret sweetness, doubly precious because of the violence outside.'

FAR LEFT: Water is especially potent in enclosed space. Here a tiny fountain refreshes the monastic calm of the cloister gardens tucked deep inside London's Westminster Abbey.

LEFT: The classic courtyard has a central focus, as in landscape gardener Harold Peto's mock-Italian Romanesque cloisters at Iford Manor, Wiltshire, built around a fourteenth-century well head and finished in 1914.

OVERLEAF: From the street all you can see of this Moroccan courtyard is a tufted palm bursting through the rooftops.

Another influence felt today is that of the monastic cloister garden, although the originals were probably more productive than decorative. Even now, the Little Cloister Garden at London's Westminster Abbey offers a pocket of calm away from the scurry of feet on worn stone flags. Swags of ivy and Virginia creeper hang down from the surrounding walls. A stone fountain of childlike proportions stands at the centre of a small lawn edged with simple planting: hostas and ferns, rosemary and rue, foxgloves and Christmas box (*Sarcococca hookeriana*), with its wintery spikes of unexpected fragrance. The gate into the garden stays sadly padlocked, so you can only stare through the railings at this vision of peace.

New Yorkers are luckier as they can walk into the exquisite Bonnefont Cloister Herb Garden at the Cloisters, an outpost of the Metropolitan Museum of Art in northern Manhattan. Paved in brick with raised beds for aromatic herbs, the tiny garden is enclosed by a high wall on one side, a gothic walkway on another, with views on the other two sides across the treetops of the park below. At the centre, four low-growing quince trees stand guard around a carved stone well-head.

If urban courtyards come out of religious traditions, roof gardens can trace their beginnings to the nostalgia of a Babylonian queen for the trees and hills of her Persian homeland. Reputedly built for his homesick wife in the sixth century BC by King Nebuchadnezzar II, the Hanging Gardens of Babylon were raised on stone vaults and watered directly from the River Euphrates by a screw pump. Laid out in stepped terraces, they are said to have brought the Queen's favourite trees to the arid desert: acacia, aspen, birch, cedar, chestnut, cypress and larch.

But after Nebuchadnezzar, and despite a lingering interest during the Italian Renaissance, the roof garden had to wait until the mid-nineteenth century for technology to catch up with inspiration. Credit goes to Carl Rabbitz, a Berlin master builder who patented a method for producing waterproof cement. Continued developments in engineering technology meant that buildings could at last take the extra strain.

Because of their location, all roof gardens are secret to some degree, if only because they are hidden from the street and access can usually be gained only through the building itself.

They are also surreal in their displacement of ordinary activities. In early twentieth-century France, French garden designer and restorer Achille Duchêne created some splendid 'Belle Epoque' terraces and roof gardens for wealthy Parisians. A sketch for an apartment building on the Boulevard Suchet shows frock-coated dancers waltzing amidst precious fountains covered with gold mosaic work: different levels accommodate gaming tables, bar, band and an illuminated garden.

Starker roof gardens and terraces became part of the modern movement, thrusting towards the sky in the radiant cities of architects like Le Corbusier as they turned conventions on their head. With Pierre Jeanneret, Le Corbusier designed the superbly surreal Beistegui rooftop in central Paris: a series of penthouse terraces leading up to a walled solarium carpeted wall-to-wall with meadow turf and furnished with rococo fireplace and dresser in cast stone. Other terraces had sliding hedges, a working camera obscura, and a limp Lawson cypress that cost its owners 550 hours of labour but died all the same. Le Corbusier himself described moving into the all-white enclosure of the solarium as a progression into silence: 'One saw only the sky and the play of clouds and the shimmering azure.'

Modern garden designers in America especially continue to push the roof garden to its limits, as if to spite the more entrenched traditions encountered on the ground. From Germany, too, comes a strong belief in the curative properties of 'green' architecture: plants that help to filter the dust and humidify the air; plants that help us breathe.

Put all these trends together and it becomes possible to realize a dream of urban flight, and to see how the impulses prompting the creation of roof gardens and courtyards converge.

FAR LEFT: A New York rooftop offers city dwellers the chance to import or invent identities. Here the hesitant greenery must thicken before it shields the roof garden from taller neighbours.

LEFT: Built above a department store and still surviving after more than 60 years, this roof garden in Kensington, London, incongruously harbours three separate gardens: English woodland, Mediterranean Spanish, and (here) formal Tudor, its intimate corners hung with wisteria and scented with myrtle and roses.

RIGHT: In hot climates, water cools and refreshes the surrounding rooms. The courtyard here is almost all pool, its hard outline softened by lush green planting and feathery mimosa.

COURTYARDS

Courtyards, by definition, slip snugly into the buildings that protect them and take their tone from the surrounding architecture. How 'secret' they are depends first of all on their enclosure, but also on how you handle the various elements. Walls, floor, planting, water and ornament can all be used to intensify the focus and therefore the experience of entering protected space. In small spaces, simplicity rather than 'busyness' will usually work best: ideas should be clear and carried through with careful attention to the detail of design and planting. But don't fall into the trap of thinking small as well – cluttering your space with small trees and stones, or a confusion of small objects. A single large pot or jar, for example, will have a much stronger impact than a host of smaller ones.

As you seek to define your focus, look first at the surrounding walls and architecture. In the world of Islam and Moorish Spain, in China and Japan, the courtyard acts as a central well, bringing light and air to surrounding rooms. In hot climates especially, the courtyard is surrounded by cool arcades, shaded but open to the elements. First glimpsed from the dark interior of the house, the courtyard's initial impression is that of vibrant light tempered by refreshing greenery and perhaps the cooling sounds of water spilling over the rim of a stone fountain. Your 'secret' garden is already here, waiting.

In many other places, by contrast, the courtyard is attached to the house on one or two sides only, requiring you to complete the walls yourself. Take care to relate their height to the human scale: in restricted spaces, a wall higher than half the width might feel claustrophobic. The monstrous 25 metre (80 foot) glass-and-iron screens erected by the fifth Duke of Portland more than a century ago around his London home might have protected his ducal privacy, but they gave his garden a dismal air.

You may want to find ways of making walls less oppressive. Trellis adds height without mass. Creepers and climbing plants introduce verticals that can be as dense as matted ivy or as delicate as the twining stems of *Actinidia kolomikta*, its leaves

LEFT: A curtain of vines protects the entrance to this simple French courtyard. Quartered by granite setts and planted with impatiens around a fountain pool, it carries echoes of the earliest paradise gardens.

RIGHT: Originally created by painter Jacques Majorelle, Yves Saint Laurent's walled garden in Marrakesh, Morocco, mimics a desert paradise through water, shade and exotic planting (*Euphorbia canariensis*, palms, bamboos and a flaming rose).

FAR RIGHT: White walls provide an excellent backdrop for the shadow-play of trees and leaves. Walled enclosures like this one can be slotted into larger gardens like Chinese puzzles.

spattered pink and white, or one of the more hesitant clematis, such as *C. florida* 'Sieboldii'. You could also experiment with screens of polycarbonate or perspex, but beware of making your garden look like an outdoor bathroom.

Walls play a special role in Chinese gardens and courtyards: whitewashed for shadows and silhouettes; rubbed with white wax to shimmer like silk; painted in soft greys that recede in morning or evening light. Or they may be pierced with moon doors and windows in fantastic shapes and metaphors, holes in the shape of flowers, fruit, leaves, fans or vases. Like archways in a garden, such openings frame views and also change the way you see things. As Maggie Keswick suggested in *The Chinese Garden*, the moon gate focuses down the eye, acting like the light-stop on a camera to intensify the framed subject.

White walls are used the world over to inject light and airiness into tight corners and basement wells. The paint or whitewash should be regularly renewed, as green slime and mould quickly destroy the illusion of sunlit space. If shade is a real problem, whitewash everything you can – tree trunks, benches, planting tubs – and introduce furniture with as little substance as possible: metalwork chairs, for instance, and plant stands to match. Walls painted in bright colours, by contrast, step forward to meet you and should be counter-balanced by equally strong planting.

If your space is large enough (at least 10 metres or 30 feet in length), and providing the garden is not overpowered by surrounding buildings, you might want to experiment by creating a courtyard-within-a-courtyard, an inner walled sanctuary with openings in the walls that permit views in and out while concealing the whole. Such fragmentary glimpses appear to enlarge the space by adding corners of mystery. Planting should be luxuriant enough to disguise the hardness of walls.

To feel absolutely private, you may need to give your courtyard an arbour or overhead shelter to block the sight lines from upper windows. A section of pergola supporting climbers and vines, or bamboo matting, will probably suffice. Finding the best place for such a shelter usually demands a compromise between desired levels of sunlight and privacy. Think, too, about how your courtyard will look from upper

floors (especially if these are your own). Japanese courtyards often contain small trees such as ornamental maples that look their best when viewed from the first floor.

If you suffer from claustrophobia, try to 'borrow' some detail from your surroundings as a way of enlarging your own space and reaching out beyond your walls. In China the technique is called '*jie jing*' (borrowing views) and '*shakkei*' in Japan (which meant originally 'a landscape captured alive'). As well as the scenery to be borrowed, you will need a capturing device in the middle ground to link the garden with its wider scenery. In a city courtyard, the capturing device might be an arrangement of trees or climbers within the perimeter wall; the frame of an arbour; a sculpture or ornament that 'calls in' the landscape beyond; or a still reflecting pool that 'catches' a patch of clouds floating across the sky. 'In Japanese, the character for sky is also the character for emptiness,' wrote Teiji Itoh in *Space and Illusion in the Japanese Garden*. 'It means both the heavens and the blank spaces that are a distinguishing trait of Oriental painting.' Where you are dwarfed by surrounding offices and

flats, all with watchful eyes, your greatest hope is to create shelter from above, under a well-tended mulberry tree, perhaps, and to draw the eye down with detail close at hand – the texture of plants or paving, or reflections in a stone trough.

This sense of focus – of concentrated energy – is what makes the enclosed courtyard one of the most secret spaces of all. Ornament in particular can take on a strange power, like the stones in Derek Jarman's Kentish garden which he likened to dolmens or standing stones. Make sure, therefore, that your choice of ornament – sculpture, pots, seats, pools and fountains – carries forward your central idea. This may be defined by culture (Moorish, Japanese, Mexican, for example), by time, by style, or simply by function (whether your courtyard is a place you enter, or one you simply regard). In any case, you will need to take account of vernacular architecture. The water tanks and glazed *azulejos* tiles of Portugal might look out of place in a red-bricked city garden or one where the stone is predominantly grey. Plain white walls, on the other hand, might

accommodate them very well. Although simplicity must be a guiding principle, I have to admit a liking for places that collect ornaments as haphazardly as plants. Entering such a courtyard is like rifling the bookshelf of a friend.

A courtyard without water is a dry and dusty affair, but I would be just as happy with a still, small pool as a fountain. The raised pool filled to the brim and overflowing into a gutter (or down the pleated sides of a Cretan pot) gives a wonderful sense of completeness and of cups brimming over. Islam and the Moorish courtyards of Spain show how water brings sound, light and life to the centre of a house, subduing the distant noises of the city as it captivates the senses. While out in the gardens of Islam, water rushes exuberantly along rills, down chutes and cascades then up into fountains; in the courtyard its role is more contemplative, whether collected in dark reflecting pools, in stone basins and sunken tanks, or trickling gently from single or tiered fountains. Features such as these are almost always placed at the centre of the courtyard as its focal point, to be enjoyed from the surrounding arcades or rooms. Sometimes a square or rectangular pool may fill the space entirely, surrounded with a meagre row of plants in pots and perhaps a shallow fountain basin set just above the paving. Water at different levels catches the light in different ways to produce a subtle play of contrasts. Reflections in water that reaches right to the brim are especially mysterious as they lack the customary frame separating the 'image' from the 'real'.

A water feature placed off-centre will inevitably draw the eye and dramatically change the way you perceive and use the space. This may work especially well in courtyards that are not entirely surrounded by other rooms. Here, you may want to place any seats with their back to the house, looking out to water and a 'planted' wall. If you don't have a pool yourself, consider the Japanese custom of hosing down the shadier parts of your courtyard as a sign of welcome to guests.

In small spaces, the quality of materials and hard surfaces takes on added importance because these help to create 'texture' and atmosphere. 'How much I long sometimes for a courtyard flagged with huge grey paving-stones,' wrote Vita Sackville-West from the mellow brick of Sissinghurst. 'I dream of it at night, and I think of it in the daytime, and I make pictures in my mind …' In a courtyard, cobbles and setts and frost-resistant bricks can all be used to create patterns that give variety. Islamic gardens especially favour abstract designs for paving materials and wall tiles: pattern provokes contemplation and helps matter to lose its solidity. The Chinese tradition, too, encourages a variety of surfaces that bring together the soft and

the hard, the *yin* and the *yang*. Polished surfaces reflect light; matt surfaces absorb it. Mirrors embedded in walls can be used to create tricks of *trompe-l'oeil*. These work well in small spaces, although I hate catching sight of myself unexpectedly, and mirrors in the city, like windows, need constant attention. Dumbarton Oaks in Washington DC has one of the most extraordinary garden tableaux: a two-dimensional trellis screen apparently arching backwards into the distance over an inlaid 'fountain' made of glistening abalone shell.

And how will you plant your courtyard? The answer will come from the kind of place it is – and the place you want it to be. Some courtyards are packed and tiered with plants in every conceivable kind of pot, from chimney pots to galvanized buckets. Others are reduced to the barest of essentials: a tree, a wall for shadows, a few aromatics in pots. I love Spanish courtyards glimpsed behind grilles, with their terracotta pots and jars grouped carelessly on the floor and nailed to the walls. Splashes of bougainvillaea and hibiscus offset the shining greens of ficus, philodendron, and delicate mimosa.

Because these are sheltered spaces, lush planting often works well, though tender plants will need additional protection in harsher climates – plumbago with its ice-blue flowers, for example, and the fragrant pure-white stars of *Hoya australis*. One north-facing courtyard near Oxford, planted mainly as a herb garden around a well-head of Verona marble, is transformed in high summer with exotics grown in Arabic pots: chunky leaves of tetrapanax, fatsia, strap-shaped clivia with trumpeted flower heads in robust shades of orange, banana, asparagus, hostas, ferns and ligularia. Enclosed on two sides by the whitewashed walls of the house, and on the other two by pleached arches of *Acer platanoides* 'Drummondii', the courtyard has deliberate echoes of a Sicilian cloister garden. Planting, too, evokes the sullen heat of Southern Italy where Arabic, Norman, Spanish and African influences flow together.

Climbing plants for a courtyard include many of those already mentioned – clematis, honeysuckle, jasmine, ivies, Virginia creeper, actinidia and trachelospermum. Tender climbers and wall shrubs may thrive in its protected microclimate – varieties such as *Fremontodendron* 'California Glory', with its showy yellow bells.

A single (deciduous) tree in a courtyard is enough to give your space a sense of unfolding seasons, from the starkness of winter to the summer's jostling green. My grandmother on my father's side had a small cherry tree in her otherwise bare, Northern backyard. She watched it constantly from her kitchen window until my grandfather cut it down without consulting her. (She never forgave him.) One of my favourite trees for a courtyard is *Stewartia pseudocamellia* with bark like rippled muscles and delicate cup-shaped flowers like large white dog roses spotted with yellow yolks. But it grows quite tall, 20 metres (66 feet) or more, and would need careful pruning to keep within bounds.

For sounds in my secret courtyard, I want only birdsong and water to distract from city noises. In his fragmentary novel *Andreas*, Hugo von Hofmannsthal described such a courtyard in Venice (where else?) enclosed by trellised walls and roofed with vines: 'The sun, shining through this roof, silhouetted the lovely design of the grape-leaves on the brick floor. In the small bower, half room, half garden, with the smell of grapes and the tepid air, the silence was so complete it was possible to hear the sound the birds made, as they hopped from one stick to another, without even taking any notice of the entrance of Andreas …'

ROOF GARDENS

Despite all the extra care they require, roof gardens offer the secret gardener one of the greatest gifts a garden can bring: the exhilaration of surprise. There's a madness to the enterprise I can only admire. I once worked for an alternative publisher at his west London home in a Georgian terrace which he had turned upside down and inside out, growing trees on the roof and building a duck pond that flowed from the garden into his ground-floor living room. Ducks could dive beneath the plate glass barrier to join the publisher and his friends seated on cushions around the kidney-shaped pool. There was only one problem, however: have you ever tried to house-train a duck?

Like the fragile nest of a bird, a roof garden demonstrates a cosmic confidence, holding out the comforts of prospect and refuge in equal measure. Perched high above the streets you can see without being seen – and if you are overlooked by other buildings, you can add screens for privacy, safety and shelter. How you treat the space will depend on whether you want to take advantage of wide city views or whether you prefer instead to block out the city entirely and imagine you are somewhere else. A London roof garden I saw recently was built into a

FAR LEFT: American architect Rick Mather pulled apart the top two floors of his house in London to drop a roof garden into its crown like a nest. Much of the planting is Mediterranean and small-leaved to survive sun and winds.

LEFT: Indoor and outdoor plants mingle through glass in this converted cardboard factory in Paris, where all rooms overlook the garden well. Outside, climbers like Virginia creeper (*Parthenocissus quinquefolia*) stretch vertically and horizontally to extend the feeling of space.

first-floor balcony. Sliding glass doors opened on to what looked like a Mexican courtyard enclosed on the other three sides with chipboard panels painted to resemble the sky, crossed by puffy clouds and fading from blue to the palest grey. Wooden decking, grasses and succulents continued the Spanish-American theme.

To make a roof garden or terrace as secret as possible, you will need to concentrate on three factors: how you carve out the space; how you screen; and how you plant. If you are building a house from scratch, your options about where and how to site a roof garden are constrained only by cost, engineering and planning law. Adapting an existing roof usually entails a compromise between what you have and what you want. You could follow the example of Rick Mather, a London-based American architect who demolished and rebuilt his roof,

creating a two-tier roof terrace that is frankly modern in its use of materials and in the way it seeks to 'marry' inside and outside. Planting has been carefully chosen to survive the drying effects of rooftop winds, with the greys, silvers and greens of the Mediterranean predominating.

Unless your terrace is cradled within a skyscape of other roofs, you will almost certainly need some form of screening. Barriers should be semi-permeable to baffle the wind – otherwise they will create unpleasant eddies or simply blow down. Stoutly constructed and anchored trellis is an obvious solution, or metal mesh safety barriers extended upwards into planting screens. You could also use high-strength polycarbonate on a framework such as scaffolding poles; the screens should be staggered slightly to deflect the wind without causing turbulence.

RIGHT: Screening materials should reflect the character of the garden they enclose. Laths of bamboo here pick up the Japanese theme, and the classically Japanese planting of bamboo, azaleas and hostas.

FAR RIGHT: Viewed in close-up pots of cacti block out the city skyline, bringing a breath of greenery to the tightest space.

Planting will depend on the kind of aerial space you want to create. Roof gardening appears to encourage extremes – from the spartan simplicity of Zen to bulging, temperate jungles or (even more surreal) the nonchalance of roof gardens planned as if they had their feet on the ground, with alleys of pleached trees and neatly tended vegetables. Good plants for screening include dogwoods, buddlejas (such as *Buddleja alternifolia*), the semi-evergreen Chilean potato tree (*Solanum crispum* 'Glasnevin') and smaller willows like the coyote willow (*Salix exigua*). Russell Page even planted the fast-growing weeping willows above a Parisian furrier, creating a walkway of rustling arches.

Each roof space creates its own microclimate, so planting rules are hard to formulate. In general, though, small-leaved plants are more likely to flourish in dry, windy conditions; and

many evergreens and variegated varieties will suffer. Roof gardeners are divided about whether to install automatic watering devices such as leaky pipes or to water by hand. Although more laborious and restricting, hand-watering means that each plant gets a regular inspection – often daily or more.

The roof gardens I most want to inhabit I have seen only in photographs. First is the vision of walled emptiness created for his own residence by the late Mexican landscape architect, Luis Barragán. The photograph is black and white. It shows a blank wall, a stretch of empty paving cut by shadows, and the borrowed view of a single tree beyond.

The next photograph is shiningly green. It shows a Brazilian roof terrace on the flat roof of a simple adobe house. Plate glass separates the terrace from the gathering jungle.

The third photograph is ambiguous. It depicts an aerial courtyard, neither of the earth nor of the sky: a square roof terrace inset into the top storey of a narrow building in a vaguely modernist style. A single date palm protrudes like a tuft of grassy hair.

'Happy rectangle; some palm trees,
jade fountains; time flows,
water sings, the stone is silent, the soul,
suspended in a moment of time, is a fountain.'
OCTAVIO PAZ, 'STANZAS FOR AN IMAGINARY GARDEN'

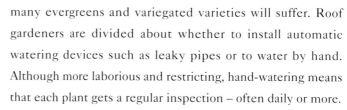

A Garden in the Sky

The raucous streets of the Faubourg Saint-Antoine in the centre of Paris conceal garden designer Camille Muller's own corner of paradise that spills over sloping roofs, climbs up and down steps and ladders, swoops inside and out, in flagrant disregard of habitual boundaries. Here the sounds are equally disorientating in a district that once rang to the cabinet-maker's hammer: a chattering of birds and the steady murmur of water dripping into pools beneath great bamboos.

Like many industrial roofscapes, this one dips into a central hollow scored with skylights and windows that bring a flood of natural light to working areas. Properly used, such a space can create a lost world at the heart of the house, protected by walls of ever-changing green. Already separated into different levels, the rooftop has been further divided by crowded planting that dissolves any sense of scale: trees such as willow, olive, peach, apple, even a giant-leaved foxglove tree (paulownia) have all been tried.

The darkest well is surrounded by clumps of the tree-like bamboo *Semiarundinaria fastuosa* that shoots upright to some 11 metres (33 feet), its leafy tufts providing a screen for a raised platform planted with grasses, juniper, heathers and pelargoniums. If you climb some more steps you reach

a wooden deck and small seating area in the delicate shade of *Elaeagnus commutata*. Pots and hanging baskets crowd the eye, planted with cypress, sumach, *Impatiens balsamina* and more colourful pelargoniums. Muller's love of detail shows, too, in his playful use of ornament: are the brightly coloured pegs for clothes or display?

Look into the 'V' of the roof and you will see jungle foliage pressed against the skylights from inside, and many more pots either suspended or carefully placed on lead shelving. Today's planting includes ferns and a fine *Nerium oleander*. But come back next year and the pots will have changed again. This garden stays fresh through constant re-invention. A good watering system is also essential, and the gutters must be kept clear of leaves. Otherwise an annual feed keeps the plants in this healthy state, with a little extra care in times of frost.

Most secret of all is the lower seating area in the bamboo forest, close by a goldfish pool with rustling fountain. Vines grown against a backcloth of ivy mean the leaf colour never stays still, from the translucent blush of early spring through the summer's solid green to the crimson reds of autumn. Here time stops still while the city drifts away like a memory.

ABOVE: Exuberant planting overwhelms but does not disguise the building's industrial past.
RIGHT: Reached through long, dark corridors, the aerial forest bursts unexpectedly on the senses. Here on the uppermost deck, seats shelter beneath a pot-grown silver berry (*Elaeagnus commutata*).

ENTRANCE
TO SITTING
ROOM

9

10

TABLE AND CHAIRS

11

LADDER

WOODEN DECK

13

7

8

STEPS

WOODEN RAIL

5

STAIRS

4

6

WINDOWS

3

12

2

GUTTER

Imaginative planting covers every surface:
at gutter level, *Nerium oleander*, lilies and
pelargoniums rise up past a slender Italian
juniper to a balcony crammed with aromatic
herbs like spiky lavender.

WINDOWS

ROOF

1

1

This upper view
shows how the areas
relate. Climbers
provide the essential
outer wrapping that
holds the design
together – Virginia
creeper, ivy and the
crimson glory vine.

14

ROOF

17

15

16

A view along the gutter towards the bamboo forest reveals more plants below the skylights. Outside, no pot rests directly on the roof.

POTS

POND   LOWER LEVEL

18

TABLE AND CHAIRS

14

18   **19**

ROOF

ROPE FOR CLIMBERS

Hidden deep in the well is a very private sitting area – entirely improbable for a roof. Birds in the bamboo and water trickling into the goldfish tank block distant city sounds.

20

KEY TO PLANTING

1 Willow (*Salix*) **2** Pelargoniums **3** Silver banner grass (*Miscanthus sacchariflorus*) **4** Ferns **5** Catalpa
6 Apple (*Malus*) **7** *Buxus microphylla* var. *japonica* **8** Azalea **9** *Elaeagnus commutata* **10** *Juniperus scopulorum* 'Skyrocket'
11 *Rhus typhina* **12** *Nerium oleander* **13** *Phyllostachys nigra* **14** *Vitis coignetiae* **15** Roses **16** Aromatic herbs
17 *Semiarundinaria fastuosa* **18** *Parthenocissus quinquefolia* **19** Ivy (*Hedera helix*) **20** *Elaeagnus* × *ebbingei*

2.5m/8ft

ABOVE: Purple foxgloves and crimson corn cockle stand colourful guard at the margins
of dark woodland.

INTO THE WILD

Tread gently the mossy steps that lead you up into the

woods, through a tunnel of twisting stems. Passing by

banks of wild flowers, remembered (or invented) from

younger days, your senses kick back to life as you step

from tamed order into the freshness of the wild.

Secret gardens slip into the wilder corners of town and country – wild in their siting and in their natural abandon. The children in Hodgson Burnett's The Secret Garden *are determined not to turn their discovery into a 'gardener's garden, all clipped an' spick an' span .... It's nicer like this with things runnin' wild, an' swingin' an' catchin' hold of each other.' But wild gardens exist also in the imagination, for city dwellers especially. As the world becomes increasingly man-made, we project on to our imagined wildernesses the myths and memories that make us who we are. And so the gardens of this chapter hark back to some of my earliest hiding places, to the woodlands and meadows of an English childhood, to jungles real and recreated. They are secret in the way all wild places are, untramped and untrammelled; and like all wild places, they bring me closer to myself.*

RIGHT: Steps in a Cornish garden curve upwards through a sinewy tunnel
of rhododendron where only children can walk unbowed.

TRADITION

'There have always been two kinds of arcadia,' wrote Simon Schama in *Landscape and Memory*, 'shaggy and smooth; dark and light; a place of bucolic leisure and a place of primitive panic.' So, too, have there always been two different ways of responding to the real wilderness – by shutting it out or by inviting it into our hearts and minds. In the Middle Ages, for instance, men built their gardens behind high walls and fences that excluded the brigands and the wolves roaming the countryside beyond. The Ancient Greeks, by contrast, used the inherent mystery of woods and groves, of wildernesses and wild meadows, to shelter secrets of their own.

Visions of Eden have swung between the two responses – at times, keeping the beasts at bay behind a stout palisade fence; at others, inviting them to wander within the charmed enclosure, as innocently as nature before the fall. Eden, it seems, is a projection of our earthly desires. 'When a Frenchman reads of the garden of Eden,' sneered Horace Walpole in

FAR LEFT: This spyhole view into wilderness offers a classic image of the lost garden. Crumbly brick and distressed wall further suggest a garden that awaits re-awakening.

LEFT: Standing stones brood like tribal totems over a private hillside garden in Maine, USA, sparely planted with birch, pine and moss.

his *History of the Modern Taste in Gardening*, 'I do not doubt but he concludes it was something approaching that of Versailles, with clipt hedges and trellis work.'

Though gardens in Europe remained relatively formal until the eighteenth century, the Italian Renaissance had encouraged a taste for little groves or boscos of evergreen oak, places of shady mystery where one could escape the rigours of geometry. In France and the great baroque gardens of Germany and Austria, these developed into *bosquets* on either side of the open parterres, ornamental groves and shrubberies that hid statues, fountains, basins, labyrinths and little pavilions according to a complex hierarchy of design.

In early seventeenth-century England, Francis Bacon proposed that princely gardens should devote at least a fifth of their acreage to a '*Natural wildnesse*', treeless but full of thickets, 'made onely of *Sweet-Briar*, and honny-suckle, and some *Wilde Vine* amongst'. He recommended little mounds planted with wild flowers and topped with clipped standards of roses, juniper, holly and gooseberry. The seventeenth century also witnessed a taste for formal 'wildernesses': radiating walks set between clipped hedges in the shape of a star, a cross or a goose-foot, where guests could experience the 'thrill' of getting lost in the wood.

A surviving example is the restored wilderness at Ham House, near London, created in the 1670s for the Duke and Duchess of Lauderdale. Wide grassy paths radiate from a central circle, contained by precise hornbeam hedges cut to shoulder height and planted at regular intervals with field maples. In several side compartments, wiggly paths wind through meadow grass towards white-painted summerhouses shaped like pepper-pots. Though the wilderness looks oddly forlorn today, a painting of *c*.1675 by Henry Danckerts shows the Lauderdales promenading in their finery, accompanied by dogs and courtiers. Gilded statues, scalloped chairs and

orange trees in tubs adorn the delicious shade where favoured guests could make contact with a nature tamed by artifice, but one that still retained a hint of mystery.

Less than fifty years later, after English landscape designer and architect William Kent had leapt the garden fence and discovered 'that all nature was a garden', the rage for 'natural' gardens took hold of eighteenth-century Europe – though hills were levelled to create the scene, and rivers dammed to form serpentine lakes. Paths began to curve through the landscape, in the Chinese style. Feathered trees flowed into the valleys, becoming shaggier as the century progressed. Arcadia stretched from Virginia in the west to Poland in the east; and philosopher Jean-Jacques Rousseau – passionate advocate of unspoilt nature, of wild flowers and grasses – came finally to rest in a Roman sarcophagus ringed with poplars, on the Marquis de Girardin's

RIGHT: At Rousham, near Oxford, William Kent created one of the earliest and most poetic of English landscape gardens that retains its magic today. Here the rill winds down to the pond while a distant faun rises from the shrubbery.

FAR RIGHT: Introducing art to nature, Quentin Bell's sculpted female figure is seen across the meadow-fringed pond at Charleston Farmhouse, East Sussex. Set outside the enclosed garden, the pond marries farmland and settlement.

landscaped estate at Ermenonville, north of Paris. And so the seeds of romanticism were sown, engendering a taste for wild and lonely places where man and woman could find their souls.

Throughout the late nineteenth and twentieth centuries, different interpretations of 'wildness' have affected the wild gardens we create for ourselves. In America especially, the myth of wilderness has captured the national psyche with its celebration of a pioneer past. The American character, it seems, was forged against the harsh and savage skies of the frontier and the shrinking wilderness became a place of national redemption. And yet – as American environmentalist Henry David Thoreau himself discovered – the journey into wilderness takes us back into ourselves, for the wildness we seek is really our own. 'It is in vain to dream of a wildness distant from ourselves,' he wrote in his journal of 1856. 'There is none such. It is the bog in our brains and bowels, the primitive vigor of Nature in us, that inspires that dream.'

Another (more obviously horticultural) way of looking at 'wilderness' concentrates on changing fashions in plants and planting design – changes that lead straight from the Victorian iconoclast William Robinson to the new perennial planting favoured especially in Germany and the Netherlands. Robinson's hugely influential *The Wild Garden* first appeared in 1870, provoked by the prevailing taste for architectural and pompously Italianate garden styles. Taking side-swipes at many of his pet dislikes (which included iron fences, bare earth, rockeries and shaving), he promoted a form of wild gardening which he defined as 'the placing of perfectly hardy exotic plants under conditions where they will thrive without further care'. Though some of his ideas (such as introducing exotic climbers into hedgerows) are considered ecologically suspect today, his celebration of native wild flowers and trees, and his approach to naturalizing hardy species, continue to influence the way we plant our wilder corners.

Not all wild gardens are secret, of course, though it is hard to imagine a secret garden that is not wild in spirit. And the discovery of truly wild places in a city comes as a shock. Their secret is that they exist at all, like the wild-flower (*heem*) parks in Holland inspired by biologist Jacques P. Thijsse, who wanted to give city dwellers – children especially – a taste of the natural world. I visited the Dr J. P. Thijssepark in Amstelveen, a lush and watery Eden on the outskirts of Amsterdam. Begun in 1940, the 'park' uses wild flowers and plants in an artificial environment that has gained, over the years, the mossy texture of 'real' woodland. Constant hand weeding keeps the invading scrub at bay but this is surely 'nature' as Nature intended: woodland glades encircled with birch, willow and crooked alder; layers of royal ferns (*Osmunda regalis*) reflected in the smoothly black waters of lakes and ponds; harebells and orchids and a matting of wild flowers.

From experiments such as these, and under the influence of German nurseryman and plant breeder Karl Foerster (1874–1970), has developed a style of planting that relies on wild perennials and natural plant associations. Gilles Clément's Garden of Movement at the Parc André-Citroën, Paris, and Rosemarie Weisse at Munich's Westpark, both offer inspiring examples of how to plant the wilder reaches of your secret garden, letting plants drift across the landscape – fennel, *Rosa moyesii* and verbascums in Paris, delphiniums, day-lilies, sedum and fountain grass at Westpark

RIGHT: Wild gardens can either pretend at 'real' wilderness, or (like Bertolt Brecht) proclaim their artifice. This Australian garden deliberately introduces man-made elements into its apparent jungle.

FAR RIGHT: A window-frame view eases the transition between cultivated and wild areas through the excellent medium of wisteria: wildly domesticated or domestically wild, depending on your point of view.

DESIGN

When I first moved to Willesden Green, a featureless part of north west London, my house had stood empty for several years. In the garden at the back, a colony of Japanese knotweed stalked towards the fence, where a massive, suckering sycamore pressed hard against a treasured oak, dripping its sooty honeydew and blocking all summer light. It had to come down, and the knotweed had to be destroyed, but all my efforts to tame the seedy urban scrub had a single aim: to give back to the garden some of the nonchalant beauty it possessed when I first saw it. Or rather, to return it – patiently and artificially – to the wild state it once enjoyed. One must tread carefully through the ironies involved.

If you want your wild garden to harbour secrets, what kind of place will it be? Space, climate, soil and temperament will all shape your decision, starting I suspect with whether you want a wildness that is native or exotic. In temperate climates, your choice of a native wild garden will hover between woodland (shade) and meadows and clearings (sun), perhaps with the introduction of a wild water or bog garden as well. Whatever sort of garden you choose, you will need encircling trees and shrubs or some form of screening to create seclusion. How you manage

the transition from 'nature' to 'culture' is crucial. Will your garden merge imperceptibly into the wild, or do you wish to add the barriers of concealment? Partial glimpses, offered and just as suddenly taken away, are often the most tantalizing of all.

For gardens with both wild and formal parts, it is usual to site the 'wild' as far away from the house as possible, so that you progress from the ordered world of architecture into the messier, unpredictable world of nature through the connecting medium of the garden. Conventions exist to be broken, however. In the 1940s, American architect and designer Charles Eames built his famous house at Pacific Palisades, California, to look out at the wild-flower meadow that was to be the original site for the house. The most intimate spaces are all clustered around the house like outdoor rooms, each with a view out to the meadow.

My own secret garden follows the norm, I must admit, by pushing the wild out to the periphery. Hidden behind bamboos and a spreading cornus I have created a small clearing beneath the towering oak (much happier now that the sycamore has gone). Here the banks run wild with daffodils and bluebells in spring, and are later self-seeded with foxgloves, borage, and other wild flowers that have chosen to live here. The space is small: no more than 6 x 9 metres (20 x 30 feet) but it feels like jostling woodland.

Two of my favourite secret city gardens adopt the same principle of placing the wild as far away from the house as possible. Both drop down from formal terraces flanked with bulging herbaceous borders. Such a marked change in level emphasizes the idea of a journey – a descent – into wildness, and keeps you hidden from the watchful eyes of the terrace at your back. In the first garden, the wildest part is encircled by a yew hedge: a sloping 'meadow' with orchard trees, a lushly planted grotto and a fenced run for chickens. You enter the second through a ceanothus arch, down some steep steps and across a slope of tussocky grass. A child's swing hangs motionless from the wide branches of a mulberry tree, reached by a path trodden through thigh-high wild flowers. Beyond the swing you can just make out a marble tablet, a seat and a stone angel. Both gardens conceal their endings by careful planting on the boundary that merges into the trees beyond, and by catching your curiosity with plants and features closer to hand.

WOODLAND GARDENS

You don't need to live in Ancient Greece to appreciate the wonder and mystery of trees, from the majesty of a single oak to the rustling of broad-leaved forests and the deathly stillness of pine woods. 'Never underestimate the value of a handsome tree,' wrote American designer Thomas Church in *Gardens are for People*. 'Protect it, build your house and garden compositions around it, for it offers you shade, shadow, pattern against the sky, protection over your house, a ceiling over your terrace.'

With luck you will already have trees that can form the basis for your woodland garden and preferably ones grown to a reasonable size. If not, you can at least decide the kind of wood you most want to evoke: northern forest, sandy heath, orchard, olive grove, or a recreated 'paradise' of delicately leaved species such as mimosa and robinia (the shrubby *Robinia hispida* is one of my favourites, its rose-pink flowers resembling suspended lupins). I never walk through Cliveden's unearthly ilex grove without thinking myself in the sacred woods of Italy, where 'colour' comes from light and shade and gradations of green.

An early choice you must make is whether to concentrate on native or imported trees. The choice affects more than aesthetics: native (and naturalized) species tend to support

FAR LEFT: Wild gardens are not for the tidy in spirit. Clustering roses (*Rosa* 'Princesse de Nassau') add a casual beauty to a decayed trunk.

LEFT: A rustic log path claims this woodland as cultivated land. Yellow spikes of *Ligularia stenocephala* brighten the many shades of green.

OVERLEAF LEFT: Contrast is all-important. At Sissinghurst, beneath the canopy of hazels, a nonchalant stone god makes the Nuttery a wilder place.

OVERLEAF RIGHT: When possible plant to take advantage of sunlight. Grasses and delicate flowers like these Welsh poppies (*Meconopsis cambrica*) turn translucent against the sun.

more varied wildlife, although birds, frogs and many insects take the exotic in their stride. In a temperate zone such as Britain, good 'native' woodland trees for gardens include silver birch (*Betula pendula*), field maple (*Acer campestre*) and rowan (*Sorbus aucuparia*); or you could introduce 'wild' blossom trees like the myrobalan plum (*Prunus cerasifera*) and hawthorn (*Crataegus monogyna*). Native evergreens are rare: exceptions include yew (*Taxus baccata*), holly (*Ilex aquifolium*), common juniper (*Juniperus communis*); and the regal Scots pine (*Pinus sylvestris*), although its eventual 20 metres (65 feet) will outgrow most gardens. More 'exotic' trees that adapt reasonably well to small and especially medium-sized gardens include the

Katsura tree (*Cercidiphyllum japonicum*); the Judas tree (*Cercis siliquastrum*), which flowers first on bare wood; *Stewartia pseudocamellia*; *Parrotia persica* (the Persian ironwood); and catalpas such as *Catalpa bignonioides* or *C. speciosa*.

Trees that drip protective screens work especially well in gardens where you want to draw a veil between different areas: weeping willow (*Salix babylonica* or more usually, *S.* × *sepulcralis* var. *chrysocoma*); the Mexican weeping pine (*Pinus patula*); maybe one of the weeping junipers such as *Juniperus rigida*; or the droopy spruce, *Picea breweriana*, although I do sometimes wish it would cheer itself up. Woodland gardens composed only of conifers can seem gloomily Victorian. I make exception for pines, such as the stone pine of Italian gardens (*Pinus pinea*) and the dwarf mountain pine (*P. mugo*). In larger gardens I hanker after plantations: a formal belt of birch trees, planted as a see-through forest; or a nut-walk as recommended by Gertrude Jekyll.

To create thickets and secret corners, you might want to underplant with small trees and shrubs (blackthorn, buckthorn and hazel, for example) or mounds of climbers such as clematis and honeysuckle allowed to ramble at will. Hazel adapts well to coppicing: cutting back the stems to within 15 to 30 centimetres (6 inches to 1 foot) of the ground every few years to encourage fresh, vigorous growth. If practised selectively, coppicing will introduce pockets of light into the woodland without destroying its mystery; and it can be used to restrain larger species such as ash, field maple, hornbeam, oak, silver birch, small-leaved lime and willow.

A broken canopy is ideal for sustaining the liveliness of shadow, one of the woodland garden's greatest attractions. An excellent model is the Nuttery at Sissinghurst, a wild copse of hazel trees that grows slowly denser as spring turns into summer. The polyanthus originally planted here have long since sickened and died and now the woodland floor harbours shade-loving geraniums, ferns, trilliums, euphorbia, epimediums, hostas, forget-me-nots and clumps of *Omphalodes cappadocica*, with its white-eyed, sky-blue flowers.

The plants you introduce will naturally depend on factors like soil, climate, available light and the kind of secret woodland you want to create. Planting in drifts will almost always work

better than parsimonious scattering: a sudden swath of snowdrops or bluebells cannot fail to catch the breath. I like simple woodland flowers best: wood anemone and lily-of-the-valley, columbine and Solomon's seal, foxgloves and sweet violets, native geraniums and euphorbias; and for deeper shade, the many varieties of fern and delicate epimediums.

William Robinson's *The Wild Garden* and Gertrude Jekyll's *Wood and Garden* remain planting classics, recommended for their style and the vigour of their opinions. Robinson's championing of plants now classed as ghastly weeds, such as Japanese knotweed and the large white bindweed, would make today's gardener turn pale. But read him for his ideas on 'dropping' plants into the wild, and for the fine illustrations by Alfred Parsons: an accident of *Myrrhis odorata* and white harebells; lianas of aristolochia engulfing a cypress; giant cow parsley and giant scabious; a white climbing rose scrambling over an old catalpa tree; Solomon's seal and herb-Paris beside a flowing stream. Jekyll I read primarily for her sharp nose and for her evident experience. I long to own a woodland garden large enough for the giant lily, *Cardiocrinum giganteum*, whose scent she described as a 'waft of incense' at fifty yards and which, by moonlight, gains 'a strangely weird dignity'.

CLEARINGS AND MEADOWS

Like American writer Michael Pollan, I am seduced by the clean simplicity of meadows. 'To look at a freshly mowed meadow path,' he wrote in *Second Nature*, 'the way it draws such a crisp, syntactical, human line through the soft and billowy heedless grass, is, I think, to understand the gift of the garden to the wilderness, and its dazzling reciprocation.' Meadows hidden within gardens are doubly seductive, like a wild-child among the mannequins.

Despite their open nature, meadows can feel surprisingly private. On a recent Saturday in June, I sat among the meadow grass of the orchard at Sissinghurst, oblivious to the other visitors who crowded the narrow paths. Here I read Harold Nicolson's letter to his wife, Vita Sackville-West, endorsing her proposals for a meadow path 'edged with musk roses and iris and winding paths in the middle with dells, boskies, tangles – in fact, scope for everything but not garden flowers – wild roses, white foxgloves in droves, narcissus in regiments …'

To be really secret, a meadow should be enclosed, by walls and trellis like the flowery meads of medieval woodcuts, or hidden within native hedgerows. Depending on where you live, this could mean a hedge of hawthorn, blackthorn, hornbeam and beech, perhaps thickened with evergreens such as holly and threaded with honeysuckle, hop and wild clematis with its popular name of traveller's joy. Or try a hedge that flowers or fruits: sweet briar (*Rosa eglanteria*), the wayfaring tree (*Viburnum lantana*), *Cotoneaster lacteus*, escallonia, berberis, or even a flowering gooseberry or redcurrant.

Most gardeners' lawns are much too fertile to grow wild flowers well and many will have been treated with moss- and weed-killers. The best advice is to strip away your existing turf and layer of top soil, then to sow a special mixture of fine grasses such as bents (*Agrostis*) and fescues (*Festuca*) mixed in with about fifteen per cent wild-flower seeds, avoiding vigorous grasses like ryegrass. Sow in early autumn for light soils and in

spring for heavy soils that may become waterlogged. Pot-grown plants or bulbs (like the speckled heads of *Fritillaria meleagris*) can be added later, or to existing grassland.

The wild-flower mixture you choose (and your maintenance regime) will depend on whether you want a spring or a summer meadow. My favourites for spring include lady's smock, bugle, daisies, cowslip, primrose and yellow rattle. For summer, my planting would include ox-eye daisies and red poppies, harebells and field scabious, musk mallow and meadow buttercup. Wherever possible, look for seed that comes from your own country, to give your meadow a higher chance of survival and to guard against introducing genetic differences that may later spread into the wild. Removing plants from the wild is often illegal and always to be discouraged.

A visit to Westpark in Munich has tempted me to experiment with wild perennial planting in a meadow setting, an approach that relies on good drainage and relatively impoverished soil. I would also want to give the 'meadow' definition and seclusion by leading it up a woodland edge. Propelled by self-seeding, loose areas of plantings float dreamily into each other – a 'natural' style of planting particularly suited to secret flower gardens where the wild and the cultivated live side-by-side.

RIGHT: A mossy stream brings light, sound and movement to a subtropical woodland, supporting abundant wildlife and a ruff of bog plants: sedge (*Carex comans*), *Soleirolia soleirolii*, *S. s.* 'Aurea', castor oil plant (*Ricinus communis*), water hyacinth (*Eichhornia crassipes*) and duckweed.

FAR RIGHT: Surprise lifts the spirits in a secret garden (any garden). A stone gargoyle appears to rise out of the rockface, peering through a scaly veil.

of some 6 x 12 metres (20 x 40 feet) can be made to feel like the deepest jungle, although you will need to curtail its itinerary. For terraced gardens, you will probably need to screen the sides (and possibly overhead) until plants and climbers are properly established. Use stout trellis, slatted wood or bamboo poles.

For the strongest effects, choose plants that flaunt their flamboyant architecture: hostas; bamboos; stately royal ferns; great flaps of banana; spiky phormiums and fan palms (*Chamaerops humilis*), hairy trunks of the Chusan palm (*Trachycarpus fortunei*), huge umbrellas of Chinese rhubarb and the even more massive *Gunnera manicata*; hot splashes of red from canna lilies and crocosmia.

Here are some effects you might want to consider:

◊ A curving path of slate or granite stepping stones set in crumbly bark, disappearing into the undergrowth.

◊ Water oozing from every pore, spurting, dripping, cascading, catching in the throats of broad-leaved plants or slithering into an unseen pool.

◊ A permanent seat in an unexpected clearing, placed to enjoy the filtered green light and the jungle's soothing calm; and decking near the pool for wooden loungers.

◊ Sculpted faces and figures half-hidden in the undergrowth, playful spirits of the place that spy on the unwary.

TEMPERATE JUNGLES

Another sort of wild garden entirely is one that introduces the exotic into the everyday – temperate jungles, whose broad leaves and dense planting hint at the real jungle's outrageous fertility. These are gardens of exploration and concealment, where you hesitate on the threshold before giant leaves swallow you whole.

My introduction to recreated jungles came early. I was ten when we returned home from Malaysia to the English Lake District, first renting a house from a Polish widow whose husband's family had created a mini-Eden in the hills above Ambleside. The grounds had a crumbling folly built around a maple tree and two dark ponds thickly surrounded with clumps of royal fern (*Osmunda regalis*). Originally heated by gas, one pond was intended for the giant tropical water lily *Victoria amazonica* and the other for rearing young crocodiles, which grew too large, however, and had to be sent away. By the time we rented the house, all that remained were the overgrown grottoes and ferneries, and bleeding tigers on the dining-room walls.

Because temperate jungles inevitably require broad-leaved plants and dense planting, making them secret is relatively easy. You don't need much space either – even a small back garden

Put all these elements together and you begin to experience the excitement and surprise of the great botanical collectors who risked their lives in pursuit of 'new' species. Though today the risks are less, the dislocation is no less real. A friend has stocked her north London garden with many of the plants she might encounter in her native New Zealand: tree ferns (*Dicksonia antarctica*); an assortment of the mightily architectural lancewood family, including *Pseudopanax crassifolius* and the weirdly toothed *P. ferox*; grasses; mimosa (*Acacia pravissima* and *A. dealbata*); the Japanese banana (*Musa basjoo*); and black bamboo (*Phyllostachys nigra*). The effect is casually unselfconscious, where the exotic brushes with the everyday (a tree fern viewed through fronds of weeping willow, for example), punctured by unexpected touches

of humour. I like especially the chubby bottom of a miniature Roman statue amid the raised planting at the far end. Every garden, we are told, should have a destination worth the journey.

Temperate jungle plants should be able to withstand the cold of winter. If you must include slightly less hardy species, avoid planting them in local frost pockets. With tender plants you will need to take extra precautions, bringing them indoors for the winter or wrapping them against the frost. Even in regions with cooler summers, many 'exotics' require constant supervision to keep within bounds. If this troubles you, plant a different sort of garden or you will be forever clipping and pruning.

And don't forget to give yourself a secret corner in which to enjoy the jungle you have made yourself. The diaries of Victorian artist Marianne North would make a good companion. After travelling the world to paint exotic landscapes and plants, she returned at the end of her life to garden in Gloucestershire. 'No life is so charming as a country one in England,' she wrote in her diary for 1886, 'and no flowers are sweeter or more lovely than the primroses, cowslips, bluebells, and violets which grow in abundance all round me here.' Dreams of Eden have a habit of turning themselves inside out.

FAR LEFT: At Heligan, Cornwall, an old water culvert hung with ivy leads into the lost valley, the most recent area to be discovered and brought back to life through patient restoration.

LEFT: A splash of day-lily (*Hemerocallis fulva*) brings colour to a woodland floor, where the varied textures of fern, bark, pebbles and stone provide the main interest.

A Backyard Jungle

Entirely hidden from the street, this small and narrow back garden enfolds you like a rainforest in the city, its bullfrog croaks and screeching insects inexplicably absent. Footsteps pad softly on black paving stones, crunching occasionally into gravel. Sharp lines of sunlight pierce the canopy overhead. Some way ahead, water sluices into a jungle pond. The houses and high-rise blocks round about have vanished.

The jungle's seemingly natural effects result from meticulous design that seeks to inflame curiosity; like a journey of exploration it promises somewhere to go, something to look at on the way, and something to hold your attention when you reach your destination – a dark pond stretching to the boundary.

Facing west to catch the afternoon sun, the first-floor decking looks on to a wall of greenery: trumpet vine, Chinese wisteria, feathery bamboos and the jungle wall beyond. Steep wooden steps lead down to a curtain of elegantly stemmed black bamboo. At the threshold you hesitate. The planting is staged and staggered like living architecture. Immediately in front, the ground rises in a mound. Here crowd the tallest trees: a magnificent eucalyptus and beyond a weeping Kashmir cypress. Palms proliferate, including species more

usually seen in botanical hothouses in northern latitudes, yet here they survive outdoors, protected only by the garden's sensational microclimate.

A stepping-stone path curves into the garden, edged with mossy stones. You must duck to avoid the lethal spikes of yucca. Now you can hear (though not yet see) the jungle stream cascading into the pond. The house at your back has disappeared. Only the planes overhead bring you back to the city. A break in the canopy brings the chance of life to a young *Acacia baileyana* and a struggling ginkgo. Rare palms and tropical plants sit happily with native ferns, a Monterey pine and even a blue juniper. (The owner is a modern-day plant hunter.)

The journey ends on hexagonal decking jutting into a jungle pond, where fish swim perkily in the depths. Having travelled less than 18 metres (60 feet) from the house, you have entered a different world. Nearly waist-deep, the pond takes up a quarter of the planted area of the garden. Its irregular outline baffles the eye, making it seem larger still. Tree ferns crowd on to a promontory that looks like an island. In dappled shade, you could sit here for hours, watching the fish in the pond or blackbirds rustling in a thick mulch of moulted bamboo leaves.

ABOVE: The jungle canopy beckons enticingly from the upper balcony of the house. Wisteria, bamboo and winged support lend a Chinese air. RIGHT: At the start of the journey, the path curves mysteriously into dense foliage, squeezing you between spiky yuccas and feathery bamboo.

As you follow the stepping-stone trail into the garden, mossy stones, wooden edging posts and shade-loving ferns maintain interest at ground level.

PATH

DECK AT FIRST
FLOOR LEVEL

STEPS

KEY TO PLANTING

1 *Phyllostachys aurea* 2 *Chamaedorea radicalis* 3 *Phyllostachys bambusoides* 'Holochrysa' 4 *Dryopteris erythrosora*

5 *Mahonia lomariifolia* 6 *Trithrinax acanthocoma* 7 *Fargesia nitida* 8 *Cycas revoluta* 9 *Trachycarpus fortunei*

10 *Cupressus torulosa* 'Cashmeriana' 11 *Phyllostachys nigra* 12 *Trachycarpus wagnerianus* 13 *Phymatosoros diversifolius*

14 *Pinus radiata* 15 *Dicksonia antarctica* 16 Bamboo (*Indocalamus latifolius*) 17 *Phyllostachys nigra* var. *henonis*

18 *Thamnocalamus crassinodus* 'Kew Beauty' 19 *Pinus nigra* (dwarf) 20 *Juniperus squamata* 'Blue Carpet'

21 *Lyonothamnus floribundus* 22 *Arenga engleri* 23 *Holboellia coriacea* 24 *Trachycarpus oreophilus* 25 *Acacia baileyana*

26 *Trachycarpus martianus* 27 *Yucca aloifolia* 28 *Eucalyptus nitens* 29 *Ligustrum japonicum* 'Rotundifolium'

A quick backwards glance: already the house is disappearing from view, hidden behind a screen of thick-stemmed bamboo (*Phyllostachys bambusoides* 'Holochrysa').

The view opens out to reveal a tranquil and secluded resting place. The hexagonal wooden decking overhangs a mysterious pool. The stones at the water's edge suggest islands, increasing the garden's sense of 'inner space'.

⓫

POND

⓯

⓮

❾

⓬

DECK

⓭

⓴

⓰

㉒

⓲

❾

⓱

⓳

㉑

At the journey's end, a jungle stream constantly circulates, bringing life to the pond and refreshing sounds to the darkest corner.

3m/10ft

ABOVE: A mirror nailed to a tree trunk plays with perceptions, opening a 'window' where
none exists.

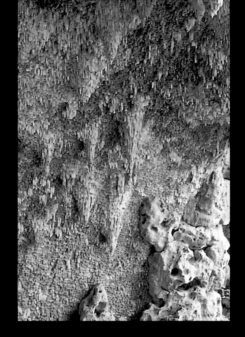

GARDENS OF MAKE-BELIEVE

The cave at first is very dark and cool, almost cold.

Water drips (unseen) from the ceiling. Moving

towards the light you bang into a sharp rock.

Turn the angle of the passageway and the cave

bursts into a shimmer of light.

The best gardens appeal to the imagination. The strict geometry of a topiary hedge snaking out of view; a sculpted stone half-hidden by whispering grasses; a trompe-l'œil *fountain seeping real water down a shell-encrusted wall: effects like these endure in the mind long after their immediate impact has dulled. So, too, do the secrets of this final chapter, which belong to the illusionist's art as much as to the gardener's craft. Drawing on traditions that go back to ancient mysteries and the eternal riddle of the sphinx, these gardens of make-believe seek to cross the invisible line between reality and fantasy, taking you into a different world where nothing is quite what it seems. Mysterious caves and grottoes that drip crystals of light, aerial treehouses, hidden dens and hideaways – here you are asked to suspend disbelief and regain the wonder of a child. Here, too, are places where children can be themselves.*

RIGHT: The vaulted grotto chamber at Painshill Park in Surrey blinds with crystal fragments reflected in the green waters of the lake.

RIGHT: At Bomarzo, near Rome, Count Orsini thoughtfully placed a stone table in the gaping jaws to the underworld, offering his guests a little light refreshment in hell.

TRADITION

The inspiration for creating secret gardens that play with fantasy and make-believe comes from many sources. The garden as site of divine mysteries, of play-acting and fun, of flight and escape into other worlds: these three traditions in particular combine to give these gardens their very special character.

We have already entered the sacred groves of the ancient world, and the shady boscos of Italy. Sometimes the tradition was distorted, as at Count Orisini's sacred grove at Bomarzo, near Rome, created in the sixteenth century and fittingly filmed in the twentieth by Salvador Dali. Bomarzo's monstrous statues tell the long-forgotten story of the mad Orlando, seen as a giant warrior ripping a woodsman limb from limb. Elephants, dragons, sphinxes, acorns and pineapples, a tower that lurches drunkenly out of line – the *sacro bosco* is a shocking jumble of grotesque images punctuated here and there with playful touches, like the English prince astride an elephant, madly stuffing poor Orlando's wits back up his nose.

The 'sacred' shades into folk tale and superstition, lending some gardens an aura of familiar strangeness (or strange familiarity?). My edition of Perrault's fairy tales contains illustrations by Gustave Doré, including several for Sleeping Beauty. The forest that grows up to hide the princess's castle is a place of tall trees and brambly thorns that part mysteriously for the king's son. The castle steps, washed in an eerie light, appear at the end of a dark avenue. Urns and balustrades give the castle an Italian air, like Fragonard's exquisite gouaches of the gardens of the Villa d'Este.

Mysteries can be found, too (though not necessarily decoded), in the allegorical conceits of the Renaissance; and in the mazes and labyrinths that seek to initiate converts into divine (or earthly) secrets. The most famous is the labyrinth at Knossos, on the Greek island of Crete, reputedly built by King Minos to house the beastly Minotaur. In Christian interpretations, too, the labyrinth represents the pilgrim's journey from perdition to salvation. Mazes today continue to present enclosure at its most stifling and a perilous journey into the heart of the mystery.

The garden has its lighter side, of course, and a long association with the theatre and with play-acting. Inigo Jones, English architect of the seventeenth century, set many of his courtly masques in sumptuously recreated Italian gardens. Water jokes and trick fountains – sometimes obscene – spread from Italy into Austria, France and Spain. At Hellbrunn, near Salzburg, water jets concealed in marble stools around the sovereign's table still drench the unwary. Throughout Europe, princes and nobles consecrated private corners of their gardens to the gods of their own amusement – most poignantly at Rambouillet near Paris, where Marie-Antoinette played in her dairy at milkmaids, until the French Revolution claimed her head.

Treehouses offered another hiding place for those wishing to escape mundane cares. Known to the Chinese, the Japanese, the Persians and the Moguls, treehouses were a regular feature of European gardens in the sixteenth and seventeenth centuries. Summer resounded to the sound of banquets held in elegantly embowered trees – in Germany, Switzerland, the Netherlands and Italy. At Pratolino near Florence (where you can still find the colossal Grotto of the Apennines by Giambologna), Grand Duke Francesco de' Medici took the trappings of the high Renaissance into the heart of a mighty holm oak, where he built a platform for fountains and marble furnishings reached by a massively ramped dual staircase.

Though later tastes stripped treehouses of such baroque flourishes, another fashion ensured their enduring popularity: the myth of the noble savage and a rash of literature extolling the virtues of primitive life. J. R. Wyss's *The Swiss Family Robinson*, Daniel Defoe's *Robinson Crusoe*, and later, the Tarzan stories by Edgar Rice Burroughs all sent men and boys (women and girls, too) back into the trees. In France, 'Robinson parks' became popular from the mid-nineteenth century, named after Robinson on the outskirts of Paris, where the bourgeoisie could dine in miniature tree pavilions, set high in the branches of magnificent chestnuts, hauling up baskets of food and drawing the curtains around their private suppers.

For me, the most fantastical secret garden of all is the grotto – a place of watery enchantments, of the mysteries of dark and light and the ultimate gateway into other worlds. Leonardo da Vinci understood its peculiar thrill. 'And after having remained

LEFT: The garden maze still jealously guards the mystery at its heart, frustrating initiates with a perilous journey of forking paths and sudden dead-ends. Reached between solid blocks of yew, the central cabinets here conceal statues and a tantalizing water jet.

RIGHT: A darkened doorway into the wings of this topiary theatre anticipates sudden exits and entrances, while the stone figure stands permanent guard.

FAR RIGHT: A stilted bower of wisteria creates a fantastical two-storied look-out over hills and woods; snapdragons and showy brugmansias line the approach.

at the entry some time, two contrary emotions arose in me, fear and desire – fear of the threatening dark grotto, desire to see whether there were any marvellous thing within it.'

Grottoes have two lines of development that continue to influence those built today: the first is the rustic cave that can be traced back to the Greeks, a place of retreat and meditation carved from stone, usually flowing with water ('an excellent habitation for a toad', snapped the more prosaic Dr Johnson). From the Romans and the Italian Renaissance extends the second line: the architectural nymphaeum dedicated to nymphs and muses and enlivened with fountains – grotto as theatre, as baroque spectacle, perfect setting for courtly entertainments, like the marbled nymphaeum at Rome's Villa Giulia, guarded by bare-breasted caryatids and protected by secret passages.

The Italians excelled at both types of grotto: the rustic cave and the marbled hall. In *Eccentric Spaces*, Robert Harbison aptly described Italian gardens as 'the creations of contradictory people who hid meanings amid the shrubbery and created caves in which to bury what couldn't stand the light. Their grottoes are populated with half-human monsters, with all the rarities of the animal world, and the encasing lava makes everything seem on

the point of turning into something else.' From the sixteenth century onwards, grottoes spread throughout the civilized world, adapted to national and individual tastes: symbolically triumphant at the court of the Sun King, Versailles; resoundingly Wagnerian at mad Ludwig's castle of Linderhof, Bavaria; esoterically neo-platonic at the Bastie d'Urfé, France; frankly erotic at West Wycombe, Buckinghamshire. In England, the eighteenth-century poet and arbiter of garden taste, Alexander Pope, built a small grotto-passageway at Twickenham, near London, linking his garden with the Thames. Here he sat for hours, locked away with his muse. Ornamented with mosaics of glass, shells and geological clippings, the grotto's walls performed like a camera obscura, catching watery reflections of woods, trees, boats and the gently flowing River Thames outside.

Of all the grottoes I have seen, my favourite is the shining cave at Painshill Park in suburban Surrey, created in the mid-eighteenth century by Charles Hamilton, whose gardening passion drove him almost to bankruptcy. The grotto is situated on an island, where a twisting path leads you down to the mouth of a cave, and your first glimpse of the dazzling interior. The roof above your head drips with crystals, tiny slivers of

RIGHT: Splashing water echoes loudly through the grotto at Stourhead, Wiltshire, home to resident river god (shown here) and sleeping nymph. The garden itself is planned as an allegory of Aeneas' journey from Troy to Rome.

CENTRE: Cave-like rooms (whether above or below ground) can be decorated with simple shells like scallops and oysters; add water and light for otherworldly effects.

FAR RIGHT: A passion for ferneries developed in the 1850s, in outdoor glens or nurtured under glass. Here the leaves of *Nephrolepis exaltata* act as a light source; in the background are *Cyrtomium falcatum* and *Soleirolia soleirolii*.

gypsum, fluorspar and orange calcite. A dark tunnel beckons. In Hamilton's day, the guide would have abandoned you here at the entrance, leaving you to find your own way inside.

The first part is easy: a chink of natural light ahead makes the tunnel seem longer than it is. The wall to your left opens into a shimmering view of the bridge; an *oeil-de-boeuf* admits light from above, heightening the tension between earth and air, black slag below, crystals above. The gardener, meanwhile, has galloped round the outside to switch on the taps so that when you finally stumble into the main chamber, blinded by sunbeams, you see the water gushing down the walls and the lake opens up to view beyond spangly stalactites. Like the distinguished visitors of earlier times, you remain in this enchanted place until you become fully sensitized. Only then do you stagger into the daylight, ready to throw yourself into the next 'scene': a mournful mausoleum at the far side of the lake.

If Painshill Park has my favourite grotto, the Désert de Retz near Paris represents for me one of the strangest secret gardens ever created: a bizarre landscape scattered with follies

created by Francois Nicolas Henry Racine, Baron de Monville, between 1774 and 1789. Abandoned at the outbreak of the French Revolution and rediscovered in the twentieth century by the Surrealists, the Désert's two decades of restoration have inevitably laid some of its ghosts to rest. But its monstrous trees and desolate shadows still provoke a disturbing sense of dislocation.

You enter the estate through a grotto of heaped rocks, past a pyramidal ice house strangled by ivy on your way towards the main house, which appears to be built in the broken stump of a colossal column. The wooded estate also hides a tartar tent on the Isle of Happiness, a temple of Pan, an open-air theatre, gothic ruins, a hermitage, obelisk and tomb. Writers throughout this century have celebrated the Désert as a victory for the forces of the irrational and the primitive over the intelligence. Colette likened it to a haunted house. André Breton and his Surrealist group posed for a photograph before one of the gates. All members of the group are wearing bald-headed masks, like showroom dummies. The door to the park is shut. 'Private property', it says (in French). 'Entry forbidden.'

RIGHT: Water in all its guises brings humour and sparkle to secret corners. This impish water spout adds a satisfying gush.

CENTRE: Inscribed stepping stones by Scottish poet, sculptor and gardener Ian Hamilton Finlay in his own garden at Little Sparta, Lanarkshire, show how gardens can be encouraged to tell their own stories.

FAR RIGHT: Tread on these stepping stones by Sonny Garcia and you stamp on his US garden's indigenous spirits.

DESIGN

There are no rules, of course, for anyone wishing to create a secret garden of make-believe. Perhaps the main lesson to be learned from past traditions is the importance of courage and vision and also (depending on your mood) the liberating effects of playfulness and humour. It is possible to make your garden tell a story and, like the Renaissance gardeners of old, designers and architects are beginning once again to introduce allegory and narrative into the structure of their gardens. Consistency is all-important: the clarity of a well-considered idea carried through into the smallest detail.

If you find a single theme too daunting, you can introduce individual elements of fantasy like special effects. Sculpture (abstract sculpture in particular) helps to concentrate the focus, bringing a sense of power and energy into hidden areas.

A mocking gargoyle glimpsed suddenly on an ivy-clad wall can give your visitors a shock. Or they may 'feel' the blank, staring eyes of a woodland god before they see its hiding place beneath the trees. Some sculptures work best in intimate spaces, rising from a skirt of textured box or set against the flowing folds of shrubs like *Sambucus racemosa* 'Tenuifolia'. Low-growing or less pervasive bamboos make excellent 'frames' for sculptures set plainly on grass; or banks of euphorbia with their architectural grace – *E. characias*, E. × *martinii* and the purply tints of *E. dulcis* 'Chameleon'. Found objects, too, like driftwood, holey stones and abandoned pieces of metal all tell stories of their own. A secret garden in a chalk pit near Brighton, Sussex, has an archway of rusting metal made from the obsolete springs and hawsers of a derelict tidal mill.

Water can be used to create some of a secret garden's most potent special effects, from 'captured' sky to the exuberance of fountains. Water brings light and life and sparkle to the deadest corner. Candles placed in niches behind artificial waterfalls lend an eastern glamour to the night-time garden. Sheets of water seen from eye-level – whether raised in tanks or viewed from sunken paths – glisten with unexpected reflections. Against a flat, shell-patterned wall, a *trompe-l'oeil* urn appears to seep water from the rim, letting it slide down the shells to collect in a lily pond below.

RIGHT: Gardens that lead you from one space to the next are especially captivating. Here a shell-encrusted window opens on to reedy waters, inviting exploration of the half-hidden summerhouse beyond.

OVERLEAF LEFT: A play den of hazel woven with wicker creates an ideal hiding place for all ages.

OVERLEAF CENTRE: The massive remains of old tree roots, dolloped like mud on an open lawn, are here transformed into a make-believe hut thatched with turf and pierced with a makeshift chimney.

OVERLEAF RIGHT: Jokes stop a garden taking itself too seriously. Sprouting willow armchairs lurk within a giant wattle enclosure.

GROTTOES

Creating a grotto requires verve, a dash of inspiration and magpie tendencies. To build apologetically is to miss the point: you can hide a grotto by artful means but you can't excuse its necessary subversion. 'To enter is the significant act;' wrote Naomi Miller in *Heavenly Caves*, 'for to enter is to acknowledge the distance between outside and inside, between reality and illusion, between nature and art.' To make a grotto of your own, you must first decide whether nature or art will take precedence. Is it the rustic cave you wish to recreate or shimmering artifice? Will you carry out the work yourself, or turn to the growing band of grotto builders and restorers (many art-school trained) who dedicate

retaining wall which holds back the upper terrace to the garden. Pumped and recycled water cunningly slides and drips over rocks embedded into the cave, its mouth crowded with shade-tolerant hostas and ferns. A flopping clump of *Fatsia japonica* and adjacent planting of ivies and climbing hydrangea (*Hydrangea petiolaris*) all contribute to the grotto's secretive air.

If you need to import stones to give your cave a more natural air, try to re-use stone from redundant features. In any case avoid rocks or stones whose removal will cause environmental damage. You can make imitation limestone or tufa by mixing one part sand, one part cement, and two parts moistened sphagnum peat. When the mixture is stiff but not completely dry, it can be applied to small-mesh chicken wire attached to a 'roof' of railway sleepers or some other sturdy frame used to create the grotto's structure.

As well as in caves and rocks, grottoes can be created in garden pavilions, niches, breeze-block structures or simply panelled into garden walls. Facing materials include stone, pebbles, flints, coal slag, crystals or shells. A fully encrusted grotto devours a monstrous quantity of shells – more than can possibly be counted. 'But seven years, a thousand shells, and ten thousand pounds are all mystic quantities that recur perpetually,' wrote Barbara Jones in her magnificently obsessive *Follies and Grottoes*. Try scouring the seaside or fish restaurants for platefuls of mussel shells, scallops, oysters or more unusual shells like abalone. The shells look best when set at an angle, giving a three-dimensional effect, and scrolled into patterns. They should be set in cement and can be coated with marine varnish so that they glisten even when dry. If your grotto needs a floor, set coloured cobbles in a pattern or adopt the eighteenth-century solution of knuckle bones and animals' teeth.

You will need to think about planting and concealing. Because of their natural association with water and shade, ferns are an obvious choice, especially delicate species like the maidenhair ferns – *Adiantum venustum* is fully hardy; another fine-leaved evergreen is *Polystichum setiferum*. Frothy sprays of self-seeded lady's mantle (*Alchemilla mollis*) make a natural setting. If you find its habits too rampant, try the smaller, neater *Alchemilla alpina* or *A. conjuncta*.

their working lives to the fashioning of dreams? Do you wish to lead unsuspecting guests by wayward paths to the entrance, or bring the grotto more obviously into the drama of your garden?

For a grotto that mimics a cave, you will need a garden set into a bank, or at least a change in level. One fairly modest grotto in London is set within a brick archway scooped out of a massive

HIDEAWAYS AND DENS

Children need their own space in a garden, though not necessarily at huge cost. The saddest play space I ever saw was a perfect treehouse reached by a child-sized ladder. When you squeezed through the opening, you saw it was quite unused. In preference to adult fantasies served to them ready-made, the children had found other corners of the garden in which they could exert their own imaginations.

As a child, I built dens in a disused quarry behind our house, lost in oak woods and rhododendron scrub. Now my son must find his own secret spaces in our more cramped city garden where wildness is a state of mind. 'It was all rather overgrown,' wrote Gertrude Jekyll of the 'shrub-wilderness' of her childhood home,

'and perhaps all the prettier, and some of the wide grassy ways were quite shady in summer. And I look back across the years and think what a fine lesson-book it was to a rather solitary child.'

Children, I am sure, look at gardens differently from adults and are much more aware of their secret possibilities. Give them a patch of their own, so that they 'own' the space: a clump of

bamboos or a shrubby corner and maybe a basic structure like a wigwam or a climbing frame that they can customize, at will. They may also want scavenged material like wood, rope, canvas, old doors, and substantial prunings. Then leave it to them. The adult role is best confined to keeping a watchful (though unobtrusive) eye on matters like safety.

Arbours and bowers naturally provide good hiding spaces, though children are rarely great respecters of plants. Dens woven out of willow are ideal: in winter, push freshly cut stems about 30 centimetres (12 inches) into the ground, first marking out a circular base and making holes with a sharp stake. The idea is to create a small dome, tying the first few stems at the peak and then weaving additional stems into this basic shape. When spring comes, the den will sprout into life, giving your children a living playhouse.

But above all, give children the chance to be themselves. For his poem 'Juliet's Garden', Charles Tomlinson took as his epigram these lines from Jean-Paul Sartre: 'I knew a little girl who would leave her garden noisily, then tiptoe back "to see what it was like when she wasn't there".'

TREEHOUSES

A treehouse touches the rawest nerve of self-preservation. Take to the trees and you're safe (never mind that bears climb, too). Here you can see without being seen. Retreat and adventure, security and escape – is it too fanciful to suggest that in the trees you rediscover the smell and the taste of liberty?

Despite their long and often illustrious history, most of the treehouses I know are ramshackle contraptions, adapted over the years and adored by their occupants of whatever age. A treehouse hidden away in a secret garden is a secret-within-a-secret; an eyrie on to a private world. Decks and walkways built among the trees have a similar attraction, raising you on to a different plane and radically altering your perspective. Life is calmer, more reflective among the ruffled leaves. Americans understand this well. 'The sky seems bluer when viewed through foliage,' wrote Thomas Church in *Gardens are for People*, 'and a vista has depth and perspective when framed by branches.'

To build your own treehouse, choose a tree that is mature, well-leafed, sturdy, and endowed with low spreading branches and trunks that fork conveniently. Oak and mature fruit trees are all ideal. Industrial wooden pallets make excellent floors, or planks nailed to a frame of seasoned wood – but beware of making the structure too heavy. Wherever possible, lash the floor to the tree with nylon rope to prevent wounding it with nails; and for safety build the house about 1.8 metres (6 feet) from the ground with stout safety rails for young children. Though private in themselves, treehouses can breach the privacy of others so take advice about the need for planning permission or the bureaucrats may take an axe to your eyrie. Later you can think about ways to make your treehouse more comfortable, although to me roughness is part of their appeal. For lighting, Italian children are said to use bottled glow-worms in the summer but most of us rely on long summer evenings or more prosaic torch batteries.

Will camouflage be necessary to make your treehouse truly secret? That depends on its surroundings – if there is plenty of interest at ground level, people rarely lift their eyes much above their noses. Rope ladders can be pulled up, like drawbridges. Or you can hide more permanent steps between hedges, trellis or bushy scrub. A treehouse in a maze offers intriguing possibilities, providing you remember the shortest route.

PREVIOUS PAGES
LEFT: A tiny house
of logs, complete
with rustic planter,
stands like a nesting
box among the trees.

PREVIOUS PAGES
CENTRE: A
makeshift ladder is
all you need to turn
a tree into a house.

PREVIOUS PAGES
RIGHT: Beached
high in a hedgerow
tree like Noah's Ark
after the Flood, this
treehouse comes
with balcony,
windows and
snaking ladder.

RIGHT: A home-
made dumb waiter
aids the practicalities
of aerial living in this
compact eyrie,
stoutly suspended
between two
adjacent trees.

LEFT: Windows (and doors) increase the pleasures of enclosure by sneaking glimpses into the next world.

Here are some hiding places and gardens of make-believe that have marked my imagination:

◊ A tiny grotto by Belinda Eade shaped like a sentry box and squeezed into a city backyard, its 'roof' created by chicken wire attached to a chair. Finished with tufa, flint, shells and coal slag, the grotto lacks only the sound of dripping water to complete the habitat for a contented toad.

◊ Another grotto in the south of France described to me by Diana Reynell, embroidered with shells and mother-of-pearl and speckled with the most delicate of ferns, a mirage of sweetness and light encountered at the end of a curving, open-roofed passageway dug deep into the ground.

◊ Sculptor Richard Harris's dark, filtered cave created from curving spruce branches and located deep in the pine woods of the Grizedale Forest, Cumbria. You enter the slatted light like a fox into its lair – or rather, you did, for now the 'cave' has been reclaimed by the silent forest.

◊ Ivan Hicks' slimy green pool at Groombridge Place, Kent, where unexplained metal objects protrude like grasping hands and late twentieth-century demons litter the woods in a Surrealist's nightmare: spiders, serpents, giant stone women discarded from another age, their eyes staring and cold.

A Treetop Walk

Up in the trees, the walkway gently sways in the faint breeze of late morning. No one can see you from below. Birds chatter all around and though you are high above the ground, you don't feel the slightest fear; rather, the liberation of walking on air.

The inspiration for this very English fantasy is in fact partly French: the adolescent memory of a rose-smothered spiral staircase glimpsed in the Bois de Boulogne, Paris, which somehow linked to the treewalk at London's Festival of Britain in 1951 – the kind of connection more usually made in dreams. This staircase is 3 metres (10 feet) tall, made in Glasgow by Thomas Allan & Co and ornately Victorian in feel. It now stands erect in a thicket of hawthorns (pink and red) backed by woodland trees.

You see it first across the empty lawn, an enigmatic invitation to climb into the trees. Does the staircase lead anywhere? Hard to say. Garlanded roses prove impossible to resist, however. Suspense and surprise guide your footsteps up the metal steps, shiningly white, where you pause for a last glimpse of the house before the trees swallow you whole.

First, the walkway leads through densely arching hawthorn then veers left into sunlight. The structure is simple, cheap and very strong: welded scaffolding poles sunk deep into the ground supporting a path of removable wooden slats. For extra safety, the sides are enclosed with netting which you scarcely see. Planting, too, is relatively simple. After the hawthorns, you pass between a flowering cherry and a flaming acer. Climbers and creepers add flowers and mass along the way: *Clematis alpina*, old-fashioned roses, white wisteria, hops and honeysuckle. The effect is casually wild: too studied an air would destroy the walkway's playful way of subverting convention. '*On the stairway of the trees, we mount.*' Crucially, the height of surrounding trees and shrubs dips up and down, leading you from sun into shadow through different forms of enclosure.

Again, the walkway bends left, this time towards a wall of Lawson cypress. You pass into the rustling shade of a tall willow drawn by the sight of two open-slatted benches, like the deck furniture of an old cargo ship, placed at the sharpest bend. The willow bark creaks where it rubs against the walkway. This is a very private place, far removed from the chattering of strangers. And when you have sat long enough, you can make your way down, pushing through hops and Bramley apples as the walkway dips gently towards ground level, over the ferny stream and the hidden stone figure of Pan.

ABOVE: First seen across an open lawn, the spiral staircase invites you to push convention aside and step lightly into the trees. RIGHT: At the walkway's curve, pressed hard against creaking willows, a simple seat creates a quiet corner for sitting and watching.

From the ground, the walkway intrigues without being intrusive. Underwalks create a second 'secret garden' below, close to a waterfall guarded by the stone god, Pan.

Throughout its length, the walkway moves in and out of enclosing trees, varying the pace and subtly altering the focus.

18

19

20

21

POOL

WATERFALL

MOUND

PAN

LAWN

22   STONE STEPS

BENCH

24

4

4

23

25

Garlanded with blush pink roses (*Rosa* 'New Dawn') and unashamedly romantic, the spiral staircase's invitation proves impossible to resist.

2

SPIRAL STAIRCASE

1

UNDERWALK

3

3m/10ft

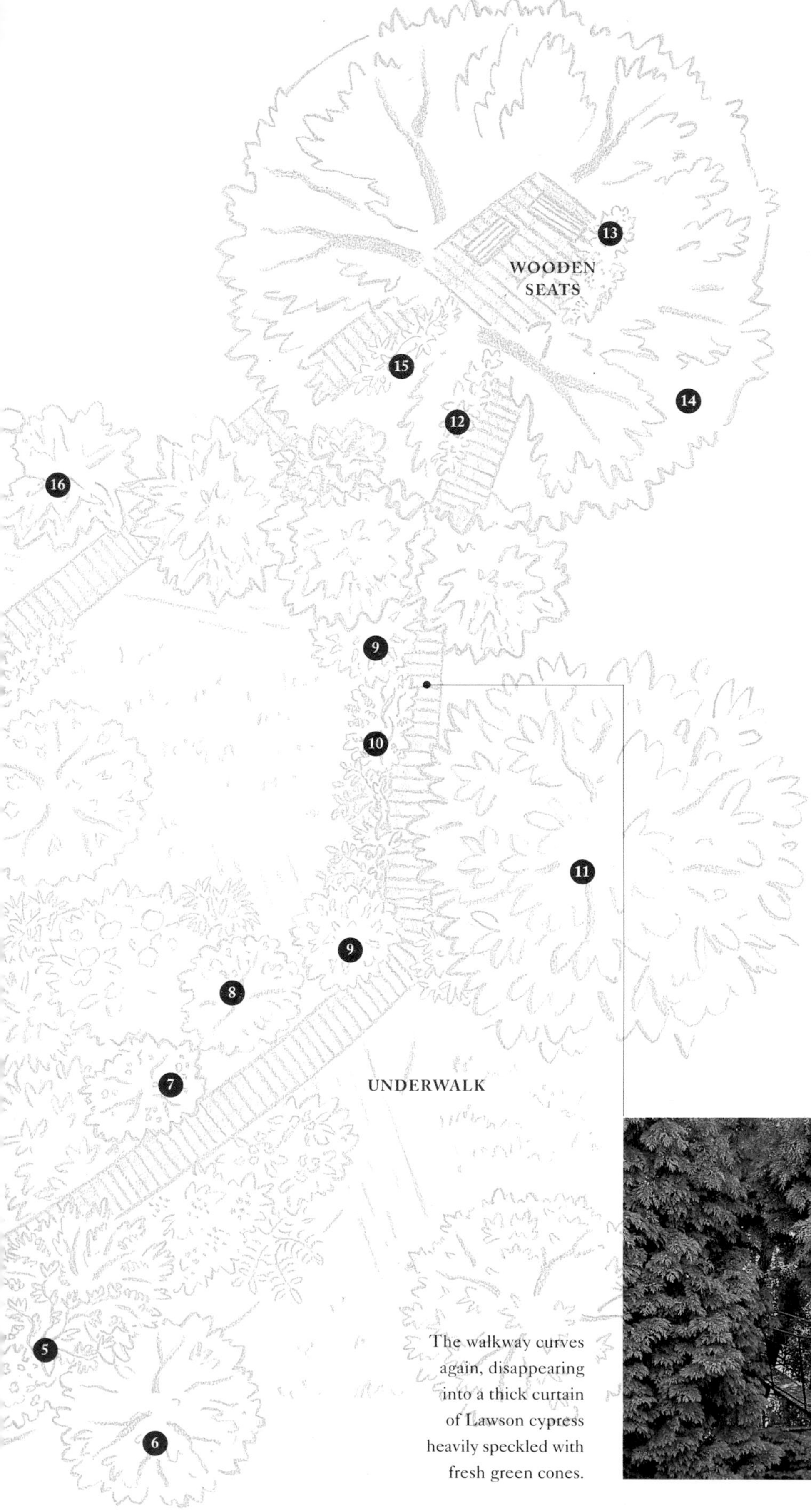

13
WOODEN SEATS
15
12
14
16
9
10
11
9
8
7
UNDERWALK
5
6

KEY TO PLANTING

1 *Rosa* 'New Dawn'

2 Red hawthorn (*Crataegus*)

3 Pink hawthorn (*Crataegus*)

4 Flowering cherries (*Prunus*)

5 *Clematis montana* 6 Cherry (*Prunus*)

7 Apple (*Malus*) 8 *Escallonia*

9 Lilac (*Syringa*) 10 White wisteria

11 Red horse-chestnut (*Aesculus* x *carnea*)

12 Virginia creeper (*Parthenocissus quinquefolia*)

13 Russian vine (*Fallopia baldschuanica*)

14 Willow (*Salix*) 15 *Clematis alpina*

16 Lawson cypress (*Chamaecyparis lawsoniana*)

17 Apple 'Bramley's Seedling'

18 Hop (*Humulus lupulus*)

19 Vine (*Vitis*)

20 Sumach (*Rhus typhina*)

21 Ginkgo (*Ginkgo biloba*)

22 Maple (*Acer*) 23 *Rosa* 'Nevada'

24 Whitebeam (*Sorbus aria*)

25 Dogwood (*Cornus*)

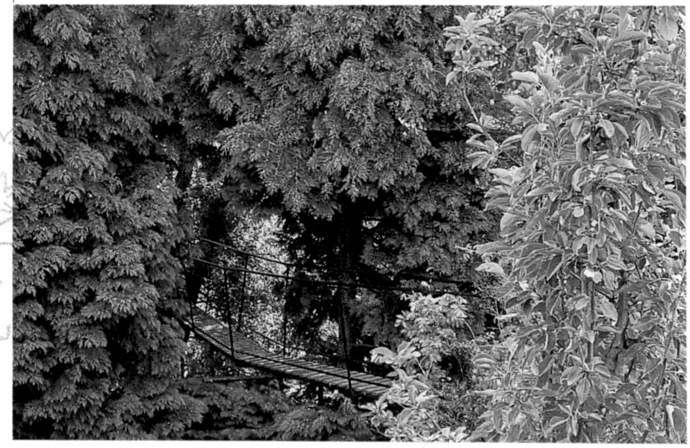

The walkway curves again, disappearing into a thick curtain of Lawson cypress heavily speckled with fresh green cones.

GUARDING THE SECRET

This book should really be dedicated to all the garden owners who agreed (sometimes regretfully) to share their secrets, as well as those who declined (also sometimes with regret) to appear in it. If every garden is to be cherished, the secret garden is at once more precious and more fragile; too many feet can trample its spirit as they mark a path to its door.

Remember the sphinx who guarded the tombs at Thebes, devouring those who failed to answer her riddle: 'Which animal has four feet in the morning, two at midday and three in the afternoon?' It was Oedipus who found the answer, poor Oedipus who killed his father and married his mother and whose name means 'sore feet'. The answer, of course, is 'Man' – the animal who crawls on all four feet in the morning; walks erect at midday; and by the afternoon of his life, hobbles on three with a stick.

The riddle of the sphinx holds a message for garden-makers that hints, I think, at why gardens are so special. For it is man himself (and woman) who lie at the heart of the garden's mystery, man the maker and breaker of riddles, the tireless seeker of magic and meaning. And the garden is where man and nature dispute their respective boundaries which shift constantly between the wild and the tamed, the 'natural' and the 'invented'. 'Good gardens,' wrote Michael Pollan in *Second Nature*, 'often seem to have this quality, of order under a certain amount of pressure, wilderness just barely contained.' How true this is of secret gardens in particular, those hidden corners that represent the wildness in each of our spirits and the tangle of our hearts.

Let the sphinx guard all your mysteries. Look after them well. Keep them hidden from those who seek to break their spell. Protect them just as fiercely from indifference. And may your garden give you back what you most desire: a privileged oasis where you can be yourself and enjoy whatever brings the greatest pleasure, whether the playing of children, the courting of youth, the caring of adulthood or the quietness of old age.

ABOVE: A locked door surrenders slowly to a crush of golden ivy. And beyond …?

PLANTS FOR SECRET GARDENS

This directory brings together over one hundred plants that are especially suited to secret gardens, either because of their beauty, fragrance or mystery, or because they embody one or more of their essential elements. *Plants for Intimate Spaces* are best enjoyed in close-up; many are exquisitely fragrant. *Plants for Screening* and *Climbers* enclose and protect a secret space. The next three sections cover *Plants for Wild Gardens: Meadows and Sun, Woodland and Shade,* and *Temperate Jungles.* Finally, *Trees* suggests some old favourites as well as species that are less familiar.

ABBREVIATIONS

(s) suitable for screening, in addition to those listed under *Plants for Screening*

(F) fragrant flowers

(A) aromatic leaves

(C) particularly suitable for growing in containers

(T) frost-tender; may need winter protection in cold areas

PLANTS FOR INTIMATE SPACES

Adiantum (C) MAIDENHAIR FERN
(evergreen ferns)
SIZE: Dependent on variety
DESCRIPTION: Delightfully delicate plants with green foliage. *A. pedatum* (40 x 20cm/16 x 8in) has branching fronds; *A. venustum* (25 x 25cm/ 10 x 10in) is similar to the houseplant maidenhair.
CULTIVATION: Cool shade and moist, well-drained soil essential.

Asplenium scolopendrium (C)
HART'S-TONGUE FERN (evergreen fern)
SIZE: 30 x 45cm (12 x 18in)
DESCRIPTION: Rosettes of glossy, strap-like leaves that bring greenery to the darkest of shaded places (or the deepest of grottoes).
CULTIVATION: Anywhere shaded that does not dry out. Happy in cracks in walls.

Chimonanthus praecox (F) WINTERSWEET
(deciduous shrub)
SIZE: 2.5 x 2.5m (8 x 8ft)
DESCRIPTION: Well-scented, little yellow flowers in late winter reprieve an otherwise rather unattractive bush. Good for cutting.
CULTIVATION: Any reasonable soil in full sun. Can be slow to flower.

Cyclamen (C) (tuberous perennials)
SIZE: 8 x 15cm (3 x 6in)
DESCRIPTION: A miniature version of the pot plant. Flowering in late summer/autumn, *C. hederifolium* is pink; its pure white form is *C. h. f. albiflorum. C. coum* flowers in mid-winter with magenta blooms; *C. repandum* is pink and spring flowering.
CULTIVATION: Well-drained soil in shade beneath deciduous trees. Tolerant of dry shade.

Daphne (F, C) (mostly evergreen shrubs)
SIZE: Dependent on variety
DESCRIPTION: Deliciously scented, slow-growing, early spring-flowering shrubs, usually with glossy foliage. Pink *D. odora* (1.5 x 1.5m/5 x 5ft) and the deciduous, deep pink *D. mezereum* (120 x 120cm/4 x 4ft) are particularly popular.

CULTIVATION: Fertile, moist but well-drained soil, preferably alkaline. Dislike being transplanted. Sun or light shade.

Dianthus (F, C) PINKS
(evergreen biennials and perennials)
SIZE: Dependent on variety
DESCRIPTION: Pink and white flowers with exquisite scent and cottage garden associations. *D. barbatus* (30 x 20cm/12 x 8in) is the sweet William, a biennial with particularly vivid flowers and strong scent. The perennial *D. gratianopolitanus* (Cheddar pink) is one of many fragrant, mat-forming species suitable for rockeries or walls. Cottage garden-style, old-fashioned pinks have wonderfully fringed and marked petals.
CULTIVATION: Full sun and well-drained, preferably limy soil. Except for the mat-forming rockery species, most are short-lived, needing propagating from cuttings every few years. Sweet Williams should be re-sown from seed every year.

Dierama pulcherrimum (C) ANGEL'S/VENUS'S
FISHING ROD (herbaceous perennial)
SIZE: 120 x 45cm (4 x 1½ft)
DESCRIPTION: Pink, bell-shaped flowers dangle on long arching stems in midsummer – exquisite and unusual. Clumps of narrow, grassy foliage.
CULTIVATION: Sun; well-drained, moist, fertile soil.

Galanthus (C) SNOWDROP (bulbous perennials)
SIZE: 8–13 x 10cm (3–5 x 4in)
DESCRIPTION: Welcomed as harbingers of spring, snowdrops vary enormously, and have attracted a cult following – 'galanthophiles' even hold snowdrop parties. *G. nivalis* is the familiar pure white form, which is simple to grow and vigorous.
CULTIVATION: Easy to naturalize in the shade of deciduous trees in thin grass. Any reasonable soil.

Hyoscyamus niger (C) HENBANE
(annual or biennial)
SIZE: 75 x 30cm (30 x 12in)
DESCRIPTION: One for the witch's garden, with its mysteriously spotted green flowers. A notoriously poisonous and hallucinogenic plant.
CULTIVATION: Sow where it is to flower in spring. Sun; any reasonable soil.

Lavandula (A, C) LAVENDER (evergreen shrubs)
SIZE: Dependent on variety
DESCRIPTION: The aromatic grey foliage of lavenders makes them ideal for planting alongside seats. *L. angustifolia* 'Hidcote' is deep blue and early summer flowering; *L. a.* 'Munstead' is later and paler (both 50 x 50cm/20 x 20in). *L. spica* (90 x 90cm/ 3 x 3ft) is late summer flowering and pale blue. *L. stoechas* subsp. *pedunculata* (75 x 90cm/2½ x 3ft) has extravagant pinky flags on the petals.
CULTIVATION: Any reasonable soil in full sun. Good in hot, dry positions and poor soil. *L. s.* subsp. *pedunculata* is slightly tender.

Lilium (F, C) LILY (bulbs)
SIZE: Dependent on variety
DESCRIPTION: Lilies have been extensively hybridized with many ill-proportioned and garish results. Yet few flowers are as elegant as the Madonna lily (*L. candidum*, 1.5m x 30cm/5 x 1ft), which has open, white, fragrant flowers in summer, while *L. regale* (1.5m x 25cm/5ft x 10in) has white trumpets with a heavy, pervasive scent, in midsummer.
CULTIVATION: Any reasonable, well-drained soil in full sun.

Magnolia stellata (F, C) (deciduous shrub)
SIZE: Slow-growing, to 2.5 x 3m (8 x 10ft)
DESCRIPTION: A dwarf magnolia with pure white

flowers in early spring. Compact habit.
CULTIVATION: Sun or light shade. Any soil that does not dry out completely. Frost can damage flowers.

Mandragora officinarum (C) MANDRAKE
(herbaceous perennial)
SIZE: 30 x 30cm (12 x 12in)
DESCRIPTION: Another witch's plant. Its roots, shaped like a human figure, are reputed to scream when pulled from the ground! Purple flowers and poisonous, orange fruit.
CULTIVATION: Any reasonable soil in full sun.

Myosotis (C) FORGET-ME-NOT (biennials)
SIZE: 30 x 30cm (12 x 12in)
DESCRIPTION: Bright blue flowers in late spring and romantic cottage garden associations make this a popular little plant. *M. sylvatica* is the most commonly grown and usually self-seeds.
CULTIVATION: Can be sown in spring where it is to flower. Any reasonable soil in sun or light shade.

Myrtus communis (A, C, T) MYRTLE
(evergreen shrub)
SIZE: 4 x 3m (13 x 10ft)
DESCRIPTION: Grown since Roman times as a symbol of fertility – the Victorians used it extensively at weddings – myrtle has aromatic leaves and small fluffy flowers in early summer.
CULTIVATION: Requires a sheltered, warm, sunny place, reaching its full size only in warm climates. Any reasonable soil.

Polianthes tuberosa (F, C, T) TUBEROSE
(tuberous perennial)
SIZE: 75 x 20cm (30 x 8in)
DESCRIPTION: Perhaps the most prized fragrance in Victorian times, the tuberose was first cultivated by the Aztecs. Spikes of creamy flowers in summer.
CULTIVATION: Must be planted in containers, kept indoors in spring and put outside in full sun only after the last frosts. Unless fed well it will not flower reliably the next year. Dry off in autumn and store in a frost-free place over winter.

Polystichum setiferum (C) (evergreen fern)
SIZE: 90 x 75cm (3 x 2½ft)
DESCRIPTION: Elegant, finely divided foliage, with shaggy brown scales on the stems. There are several forms with even more divided fronds but these plants tend to be smaller.
CULTIVATION: More tolerant of dry soil than most ferns. Shade or full sun, if the soil is not too dry.

Sarcococca (F) (evergreen shrubs)
SIZE: 90 x 75cm (3 x 2½ft)
DESCRIPTION: Neat little shrubs with tiny, exquisitely scented creamy flowers borne, and much appreciated, in winter. Dark, glossy leaves.
CULTIVATION: Moist but well-drained, humus-rich soils; light shade.

Thymus (A, C) THYME (evergreen dwarf shrubs)
SIZE: Dependent on variety
DESCRIPTION: Tiny leaves; aromatic when crushed. Creeping varieties, such as *T. caespititius* and *T. serpyllum* (both 5 x 30cm/2 x 12in), can be grown in between paving slabs. Larger forms, such as *T. vulgaris* (25 x 30cm/10 x 12in), often feature in herb gardens. Mauve flowers in early summer.
CULTIVATION: Full sun and well-drained soil essential. Good for dry sites.

Viola (F, C) VIOLET
(herbaceous perennials)
SIZE: To 10 x 30cm (4 x 12in)
DESCRIPTION: Petite plants with spring-borne flowers in a variety of colours, although many

hybrids can flower at any time. The sweet violet (*V. odorata*), mauve or white and heavily fragrant, was a Victorian favourite.
CULTIVATION: Fertile, well-drained soil that does not dry out, in light shade or sun.

PLANTS FOR SCREENING

Bamboos (C) (evergreen grasses)
SIZE: Dependent on species
DESCRIPTION: Few plants are as useful for the secret garden as bamboos: their elegant foliage is guaranteed to create a mysterious atmosphere. Of the many species available, *Phyllostachys nigra* (5m x 90cm/16 x 3ft) is sought after for its black stems, and *Chusquea culeou* (8 x 2m/26 x 6½ft) for its gracefully arching clumps. *Fargesia murieliae* (4m x 90cm/13 x 3ft) is an especially elegant species, both for its foliage and habit. *F. nitida* is very similar. Species of indocalamus (2 x 1.5m/6½ x 5ft) are useful for their large leaves which give them a tropical appearance. *Sasa* species are best avoided as they are aggressive spreaders.
CULTIVATION: Easy in light shade and well-drained but constantly moist soils. They hate wind and drought. Most species are hardy, but check first if you live in a cold area.

Buddleja davidii (C) BUTTERFLY BUSH (deciduous shrub)
SIZE: 3 x 2.5m (10 x 8ft)
DESCRIPTION: Rapidly growing shrub whose arching branches bear purple flowers, much loved by butterflies, in summer. White, red and pink varieties available. *B. d.* 'Nanho Purple' (1.5 x 1.5m/5 x 5ft) is more suitable for small gardens.
CULTIVATION: Any sunny site and soil, including rubble. Prune ruthlessly after flowering, if necessary.

Buxus sempervirens (A, C) BOX (evergreen shrub or tree)
SIZE: Slow-growing, to 5 x 5m (16 x 16ft)
DESCRIPTION: One of the most valuable hedging plants and an essential component of the classical *giardino segreto*. Dark, rounded foliage, aromatic in the sun, forms a dense crown, making it perfect for clipping and, hence, for topiary. For dwarf form *B. s.* 'Suffruticosa' to 75 x 75cm (2½ x 2½ft).
CULTIVATION: Fertile, well-drained soil; sun or light shade.

Camellia (C) (evergreen shrubs)
SIZE: 10 x 8m (33 x 26ft) in mild climates; much lower elsewhere
DESCRIPTION: Glossy leaves and early flowers in shades of pink or white. Favourites for classic Chinese gardens. *C.* x *williamsii* varieties are often the most reliable. *C. sasanqua* is winter flowering, fragrant, but less hardy.
CULTIVATION: Hardy, but buds easily damaged by frost, so plant out of the early morning sun. Light shade, well-drained but moist soils. Good in containers, provided they are not allowed to dry out.

Carpenteria californica (F, T) (evergreen shrub)
SIZE: 1.5 x 1.5m (5 x 5ft)
DESCRIPTION: Large, white, fragrant flowers in summer on a compact bush with dark green foliage.
CULTIVATION: Any well-drained soil; full sun in a sheltered spot.

Carpinus betulus HORNBEAM (deciduous tree)
SIZE: 25 x 20m (80 x 65ft), if grown as a tree
DESCRIPTION: With its pleated leaves, hornbeam makes a popular and rather superior hedging plant.
CULTIVATION: Fertile, well-drained soil; full sun.

Ceanothus (mostly evergreen shrubs)
SIZE: Dependent on variety
DESCRIPTION: Vivid blue flowers against dark foliage in early summer or, in a few cases, such as *C.* 'Autumnal Blue', in late summer. *C.* 'Delight', *C. impressus* and *C. thyrsiflorus* are among the hardiest. All the above grow to 4 x 4m (13 x 13ft), but there are several dwarf, spreading forms as well.
CULTIVATION: Very fast-growing but rather short-lived. Need full sun and sheltered conditions. Best in poor, dry soils.

Choisya ternata (F, A) MEXICAN ORANGE BLOSSOM (evergreen shrub)
SIZE: 3 x 3m (10 x 10ft)
DESCRIPTION: Glossy, evergreen leaves, aromatic when crushed. White, fragrant flowers in late spring.
CULTIVATION: Full sun; any reasonable soil.

Cistus (A) (evergreen shrubs)
SIZE: Dependent on variety
DESCRIPTION: Papery blooms adorn these quintessentially Mediterranean shrubs in early summer. *C.* x *cyprius* (1.5 x 1.5m/5 x 5ft) has large, white flowers. *C.* 'Silver Pink' is one of the best smaller-growing forms (60cm x 1.5m/2 x 5ft).
CULTIVATION: Full sun and shelter essential. Good in poor, dry soils. Hardiness varies between species.

Cytisus battandieri (F) PINEAPPLE BROOM (evergreen shrub)
SIZE: 5 x 5m (15 x 15ft), in mild areas
DESCRIPTION: Pineapple-scented, yellow flowers in early summer. Silvery foliage.
CULTIVATION: Best grown as a wall shrub in full sun in most areas. Well-drained soil. Avoid wind and thin soils.

Escallonia (evergreen shrubs)
SIZE: 3 x 3m (10 x 10ft)
DESCRIPTION: Small, dense, glossy leaves and vigorous growth make escallonias good hedging shrubs. *E.* 'Donard Seedling' has small dark red flowers, while *E.* 'Apple Blossom' has pink flowers; white varieties exist but they are easily disfigured by the dead brown flowers.
CULTIVATION: Any well-drained but never dry soil. Sun or light shade. Best in mild and maritime climates. Cold winter winds will cause damage.

Osmanthus x burkwoodii (F) (evergreen shrub)
SIZE: 4 x 4m (13 x 13ft)
DESCRIPTION: Headily fragrant, white flowers in spring. Dark, glossy leaves.
CULTIVATION: Any reasonable soil, including thin and limy. Full sun but also does well in shade.

Philadelphus (F) MOCK ORANGE (deciduous shrubs)
SIZE: Some varieties can reach 4 x 4m (13 x 13ft)
DESCRIPTION: Rich perfume, especially strong in the evening, from creamy flowers in early summer. Double varieties have a longer flowering season. *P.* 'Manteau d'Hermine' is a useful dwarf double (120 x 120cm/4 x 4ft) whilst *P.* 'Avalanche' is one of the more refined full-size varieties.
CULTIVATION: Sun or half shade; most soils. Very vigorous so need space, or pruning after flowering.

Pittosporum (C, T) (evergreen shrubs)
SIZE: 5 x 3m (16 x 10ft), in mild areas
DESCRIPTION: *Pittosporum tobira* has scented, white flowers in midsummer; glossy leaves. *P. tenuifolium* (T) 6 x 3m (20 x 10ft) makes a fine small tree in mild localities. Several varieties with coloured leaves are also available.
CULTIVATION: Good in mild, maritime areas; resistant to westerly winds. Elsewhere, best as a wall shrub. Full sun; any reasonable soil.

Rhododendron (F, C) (evergreen shrubs; or, if deciduous, referred to as azaleas)
SIZE: Dependent on variety
DESCRIPTION: Large rhododendrons give an air of mystery to many old gardens. They can, however, also overwhelm with their funereal foliage and the dense shade they make. Large-leaved species, such as *R. sinogrande* (4 x 4m/13 x 13ft), create an exotic atmosphere in the mild climates where they thrive. Good foliage, sometimes covered with dense brown fluff, and peeling cinnamon bark are strong features of some. Brilliantly coloured, evergreen Japanese azaleas (1.5 x 1.5m/5 x 5ft), with their layered branches, are useful in the smaller garden, and can be trimmed to shape, oriental-style. Larger azaleas, notably Ghent hybrids (2 x 3m/6½ x 10ft), have the most sensuous of perfumes when they flower in early summer.
CULTIVATION: Lime-free soil essential for most. Slightly moist but well-drained soils vital. Sun or light shade. Good in containers, provided they are never allowed to dry out.

Ribes (F) FLOWERING CURRANT (deciduous shrubs)
SIZE: 2.5 x 2.5m (8 x 8ft)
DESCRIPTION: Usefully upright habit and early flowering; most varieties are pink or red (*R. sanguineum*). *R.* x *gordonianum* is pale yellow and pink; *R. odoratum* is yellow and scented.
CULTIVATION: Any reasonable soil in sun or light shade.

Rosa (F) ROSE (deciduous or semi-evergreen shrubs)
SIZE: Dependent on variety
DESCRIPTION: Roses have been a vital part of many secret gardens throughout history, loved for their scent as much as for their beautiful flowers in a wide range of colours. Given the vast number of varieties, and the dubious quality of many, selecting the right ones is vital. Old-fashioned shrub roses with their petal-packed flowers and luxurious perfumes are far more subtle than the generally garish and scentless modern varieties. As a general rule, avoid Hybrid Teas like the plague and be cautious with Floribundas. Concentrate on the following categories: Alba, Gallica, Moss, Hybrid Perpetual, Portland and Bourbon. The last three categories flower throughout the summer, the others only in early summer. Rugosa roses are somewhat coarse but useful for growing in difficult conditions, and for their crop of autumn hips.
CULTIVATION: Deep, fertile soils; heavy clays suit roses well. Trying to grow them in thin, dry or poor soils is often pointless. Full sun.

Taxus baccata YEW (evergreen tree)
SIZE: Slow-growing, 15 x 5m (50 x 16ft) unless cut
DESCRIPTION: An important hedging plant, yew has dark green needles and a densely branching habit. Older plants may carry red berries in autumn.
CULTIVATION: Thrives in well-drained, fertile soils, but is tolerant of thin, alkaline ones. Prefers sun or light shade.

Viburnum (F) (deciduous and evergreen shrubs)
SIZE: Those mentioned below are slow-growing, to 2 x 2m (6½ x 6½ft)
DESCRIPTION: Sumptuous fragrance is perhaps the first reason to grow *V. carlesii* and *V.* x *carlcephalum*, which have white flowers in early summer. *V.* x *bodnantense* 'Dawn' has small, pink, scented flowers in winter. *V.* x *burkwoodii* has fragrant, white flowers in early spring.
CULTIVATION: Any reasonable soil in full sun or light shade.

CLIMBERS

Actinidia deliciosa (S) KIWI FRUIT
(deciduous twining climber)
SIZE: 12 x 12m (40 x 40ft)
DESCRIPTION: Huge leaves give this strong grower a tropical look. Do not expect fruit unless you have both male and female plants (and few gardens will have room for both!).
CULTIVATION: Any reasonable soil in full sun or shade. Avoid very cold areas.

Akebia quinata (S, F)
(deciduous twining climber)
SIZE: Fast-growing, to 5 x 10m (16 x 33ft)
DESCRIPTION: Attractive, light green leaves divided into five leaflets, and enigmatic, fragrant, maroon flowers in spring.
CULTIVATION: Any reasonable soil; light shade preferred.

Clematis (C) (mostly deciduous twining climbers)
SIZE: Dependent on variety
DESCRIPTION: *C. armandii* (7 x 7m/23 x 23ft) has wonderfully exotic-looking, evergreen foliage with blush-white flowers in spring; *C. montana* (12 x 12m/40 x 40ft) is a strong grower with pink flowers in late spring; *C. tangutica* and *C. tibetana* subsp. *vernayi* (5 x 5m/16 x 16ft) are both summer and autumn flowering with unusual thick-petalled, yellow flowers and soft, textured foliage. All these make good screening plants, too. *C. cirrhosa* (3 x 3m/10 x 10ft) has very early, pale yellow flowers spotted purple – perfect for a winter surprise.
CULTIVATION: Shade for the roots and sun for the tops. Fertile soil is appreciated. Most dislike drought and wind.

Hedera (S) IVY
(self-clinging evergreen climbers)
SIZE: 8 x 8m (26 x 26ft)
DESCRIPTION: Useful for screening and covering walls for a romantic, gothic look. *H. helix* is the hardy common ivy with numerous variegated and other forms. *H. h.* 'Parsley Crested' has parsley-like foliage whilst *H. h.* 'Sagittifolia' has elegant, narrow leaves. *H. canariensis* looks more tropical, with large floppy leaves, and is especially good for screening although it dislikes cold winds.
CULTIVATION: Any soil, except severely drought-prone; sun or shade. Can be grown up wire netting to make a Victorian-style 'fedge' (hedge/fence).

Jasminum (F, C) JASMINE
(deciduous climbers and shrubs)
SIZE: Dependent on variety
DESCRIPTION: Sweetly fragrant and reliable, jasmines are almost essential for secret retreats. *J. officinale* (11 x 11m/36 x 36ft) is white-flowered in summer; *J. nudiflorum* (3 x 4m/10 x 13ft) is yellow and winter flowering.
CULTIVATION: Any reasonable soil; sun or light shade. *J. nudiflorum* is especially tolerant of poor soil, shade and exposure.

Lonicera (S, F) HONEYSUCKLE
(mostly deciduous twining climbers)
SIZE: Dependent on variety
DESCRIPTION: Adored for their scent, but beware, as some do not have any! *L. periclymenum* varieties (6 x 6m/20 x 20ft) are the classic forms, with cream and pink flowers in summer. *L. x americana* (7 x 7m/23 x 23ft) and *L. caprifolium* (5 x 5m/16 x 16ft) are similar. *L. japonica* (10 x 10m/33 x 33ft) has good fragrance but can be dangerously rampant. All are summer flowering.
CULTIVATION: Any reasonably fertile soil that does not dry out. Sun or light shade.

Parthenocissus (S) VIRGINIA CREEPER AND OTHERS
(deciduous self-clinging climbers)
SIZE: 10 x 10m (33 x 33ft)
DESCRIPTION: Distinctive foliage, autumn colour and a self-clinging habit make them useful for adding a patina of age to buildings. *P. quinquefolia* is the classic Virginia creeper. *P. henryana* is the finest.
CULTIVATION: Any reasonable soil that does not dry out. Sun or light shade.

Passiflora caerulea (S) PASSION FLOWER
(deciduous climber with tendrils)
SIZE: 6 x 6m (20 x 20ft) in warm spots
DESCRIPTION: Often grown for the evocative name alone, its exotic, if rather wan, greenish-blue flowers are borne in summer, followed by orange fruit. Good for hot, sunny walls.
CULTIVATION: Any reasonable soil. Full sun and shelter are important. Dislikes cold climates.

Rosa (F) CLIMBING AND RAMBLER ROSES
(deciduous thorned climbers)
SIZE: Dependent on variety
DESCRIPTION: Old-fashioned varieties are usually judged the most romantic, but if you want flowers all summer, select a 'continual' or 'remontant' (repeat) flowering variety. Rambler roses are large (6 x 6m/20 x 20ft) and flower once, in early summer. Some larger forms, such as 'Paul's Himalayan Musk', 'Rambling Rector' and *R. filipes* 'Kiftsgate' can reach 9m (30ft); when allowed to grow into large, old trees they are magnificent, flowering in early summer with vast swags of pendent blossom. *R. banksiae* 'Lutea' (6 x 3m/20 x 10ft) is a fragrant, pale yellow or white climber for sheltered, warm walls. Many uncultivated species are also available and make good garden plants for a wild look, although they flower only in early summer.
CULTIVATION: Fertile, deep soil in full sun, although the large growers can be started off in shade. Roses climb with their thorns, rather than by twining, so need tying in to a support, such as a trellis, when the growth is young and supple.

Trachelospermum (F, C, T)
(evergreen twining climbers)
SIZE: 4 x 4m (13 x 13ft)
DESCRIPTION: Deliciously fragrant creamy flowers and glossy evergreen leaves.
CULTIVATION: Any reasonable soil in sun or light shade. Warm sheltered spots only as easily damaged by wind and frost.

Vitis (S) VINE
(deciduous climbers with tendrils)
SIZE: Dependent on variety; fast-growing
DESCRIPTION: Ornamental vines make good screening foliage plants. *V.* 'Brant' (9 x 9m/30 x 30ft) is an edible grape variety with purple foliage in autumn; *V. coignetiae* (12 x 12m/40 x 40ft) is a fast-growing liana suitable for high walls or trees. Large, rough-textured leaves with a vivid autumn colour. A traditional subject for painting in Japan.
CULTIVATION: Any reasonable soil. Sun.

Wisteria (F)
(deciduous twining climbers)
SIZE: 15 x 15m (50 x 50ft)
DESCRIPTION: Pendent, mauve-blue, 'pea' flowers in early summer and distinctive pale leaves make this a favourite climber, but it needs adequate space. *W. sinensis* is the most widely grown; *W. floribunda* 'Macrobotrys' has exceptionally long bunches of flowers.
CULTIVATION: Any reasonable soil in sun. Plants can take many years to flower well; advice should be sought on pruning to hasten blooming.

PLANTS FOR WILD GARDENS: MEADOWS AND SUN

Borago officinalis (C) BORAGE (biennial)
SIZE: 75 x 30cm (30 x 12in)
DESCRIPTION: Five-petalled flowers of the purest blue, scattered among large, coarsely hairy leaves. Used in herbal medicine as an anti-depressant. Looks marvellous with red poppies.
CULTIVATION: Any sunny site, including poor soils. Dies after flowering but usually self-seeds.

Campanula rotundifolia (C) HAREBELL, SCOTTISH BLUEBELL (herbaceous perennial)
SIZE: 20 x 30cm (8 x 12in)
DESCRIPTION: Blue 'thimbles' can be used to dot turf in summer; ideally planted alongside bird's-foot trefoil, wild thyme and other dwarf wild flowers.
CULTIVATION: Dislikes the competition of stronger growers on fertile soils. Thrives in thin grass on poor, dry soils, on rubble banks or rockeries.

Cardamine pratensis (C) LADY'S SMOCK, CUCKOO FLOWER (herbaceous perennial)
SIZE: 30 x 10cm (12 x 4in)
DESCRIPTION: Flowers of the palest mauve adorn wet meadows in spring. Needs to be grown *en masse* to be appreciated fully.
CULTIVATION: Needs damp, poor grassland, or could be mixed with cowslips in a border.

Centaurea KNAPWEED (herbaceous perennials)
SIZE: 75 x 45cm (2½ x 1½ft)
DESCRIPTION: Familiar midsummer wild flowers with pinky-mauve heads. *C. nigra* has an abundance of small flowers and is easy to grow; *C. scabiosa* and *C. jacea* are showier.
CULTIVATION: Full sun. *C. scabiosa* prefers dry alkaline soils, *C. jacea* more moist soils. All grow well in grass.

Cephalaria gigantea (herbaceous perennial)
SIZE: 2m x 90cm (6½ x 3ft)
DESCRIPTION: Primrose yellow is a rare colour on such a large plant. Useful as a wild garden plant but a bit overwhelming for the smaller border.
CULTIVATION: Any reasonable soil, although fertile is the best. Sun.

Chaerophyllum hirsutum 'Roseum'
(herbaceous perennial)
SIZE: 60 x 30cm (2ft x 12in)
DESCRIPTION: Delicate pink-flowered 'cow parsley' with feathery foliage. Long flowering season.
CULTIVATION: Any reasonable soil in sun or light shade.

Fritillaria meleagris (C) SNAKE'S HEAD FRITILLARY
(bulbous perennial)
SIZE: 35 x 10cm (14 x 4in)
DESCRIPTION: Unusual chequerboard-patterned, mauve flowers in late spring. Best grown *en masse*.
CULTIVATION: Any reasonable soil. Can be naturalized in grass. One of the few bulbs to flourish in damp, but not waterlogged, ground.

Geranium pratense MEADOW CRANE'S-BILL
(herbaceous perennial)
SIZE: 75 x 45cm (2½ x 1½ft)
DESCRIPTION: Mauve-blue flowers in midsummer on upright-growing stems.
CULTIVATION: Easy to establish in grass, especially in alkaline soils. Full sun.

Iris (C) (herbaceous perennials)
SIZE: Dependent on variety
DESCRIPTION: Incomparably elegant and colourful, irises flower in early summer. *I. germanica* and

its vast number of hybrids (the bearded irises), which come in a wide range of colours, have broad grey leaves; varieties can be 15–90 x 40cm (6in–3ft x 16in). There are also many varieties of *I. ensata* (Japanese water iris, 60–90 x 40cm/2–3ft x 16in), in shades of purple. *I. sibirica* varieties (60–120cm x 40cm/2–4ft x 16in) with blue and violet flowers are the easiest for a wide range of conditions.
CULTIVATION: *I. germanica* types need full sun, well-drained or dry soil, and to be grown without competition from surrounding plants; *I. ensata*, light shade, and moist acid soil. *I. sibirica* is happy in any soil that does not dry out completely.

Papaver rhoeas (C) WILD POPPY (annual)
SIZE: 40 x 30cm (16 x 12in)
DESCRIPTION: Short-lived, vivid red, summer flowers evoke cornfields of the past.
CULTIVATION: Any soil that is not waterlogged. Sow where it is to flower. Erratic germination, but if the soil is cultivated once a year, it will self-seed.

Stipa (C) (grasses)
SIZE: Dependent on variety
DESCRIPTION: Grasses with wispy flower/seed heads which are useful for creating a romantic look. *S. gigantea* (2 x 1.5m/6½ x 5ft) has vast sprays of oat-like panicles but occupies surprisingly little space. *S. capillata*, *S. pennata* and *S. tenuifolia* (around 40 x 30cm/16 x 12in) are denser and softer in appearance. *S. calamagrostis*, also known as *Achnatherum calamagrostis* (120 x 75cm/4 x 2½ft), has masses of soft billowing flower/seed heads in late summer and autumn, which continue to look good well into the winter.
CULTIVATION: Full sun; well-drained soil, dry sites. Unsuitable for combining with more vigorous grasses.

Thalictrum MEADOW RUE (herbaceous perennials)
SIZE: Dependent on species; those mentioned below are 1.2–1.5m x 40cm (4–5ft x 16in)
DESCRIPTION: Flowers and foliage of the utmost delicacy. Pink-mauve and fluffy flowers. Erect habit. *T. aquilegiifolium* is the most common; *T. rochebruneanum* and *T. delavayi* are very refined.
CULTIVATION: Full sun or light shade; fertile, preferably moist soils.

PLANTS FOR WILD GARDENS:
WOODLAND AND SHADE

Cardiocrinum giganteum (F)
HIMALAYAN GIANT LILY (bulb)
SIZE: 2m x 75cm (6½ x 2½ft)
DESCRIPTION: Breathtaking. Vast white trumpets hang from towering stems in early summer.
CULTIVATION: Humus-rich woodland soils that never dry out. After flowering, it breaks into small bulbs which will then take several years to flower.

Digitalis FOXGLOVE
(herbaceous perennials or biennials)
SIZE: 1.5m x 40cm (5ft x 16in)
DESCRIPTION: *D. purpurea* produces a blaze of purple-pink bells in early summer. Grow as many together as you can for full effect. The white form is icily spectacular *en masse*. *D. x mertonensis* is a more subtle shade of crushed strawberry.
CULTIVATION: Any reasonable soil in sun or light shade. Short-lived but will usually self-seed if the soil is raked over in autumn. Best on acid soils.

Dryopteris (C) (mostly deciduous ferns)
SIZE: Dependent on variety
DESCRIPTION: The male fern (*D. filix-mas*, 90 x 90cm/3 x 3ft) is a coarse but reliable semi-evergreen fern for woodland, including dry soil.

The other more elegant species, such as the deciduous *D. erythrosora* (60 x 45cm/2 x 1½ft), with its bronze-tinted young fronds, need a more moist soil.
CULTIVATION: Light or full shade. Best in moist, but not wet, soil.

Geranium (C) HARDY GERANIUM, CRANE'S-BILL (herbaceous perennials)
SIZE: Dependent on variety
DESCRIPTION: Easy-to-please and free-flowering perennials which are useful for underplanting among trees and shrubs, or as wild garden or border plants. *G. endressii* and *G. x oxonianum* varieties (30–45 x 45–75cm/1–1½ft x 1½–2½ft) have pink flowers from early summer onwards and are excellent weed-suppressors. There are many other species.
CULTIVATION: Sun or shade for most species. Any soil that is not dry or waterlogged for long periods.

Moss (C)
DESCRIPTION: Although not usually encouraged by gardeners, moss is very beautiful in a woodland setting – as Japanese gardeners recognized long ago. It combines well with spring bulbs.
CULTIVATION: Essential prerequisites are moist shade and being left undisturbed. Moss is grown most effectively at the expense of other vegetation by continued application of an (extremely safe) glyphosate-based weedkiller. Alternatively, hand pick all weed seedlings as they appear, and the moss will begin to take over.

Polygonatum multiflorum (C) SOLOMON'S SEAL (herbaceous perennial)
SIZE: 90 x 30cm (3 x 1ft)
DESCRIPTION: Elegant arching foliage with small, pendent, cream flowers in late spring.
CULTIVATION: Any well-drained soil that does not dry out. Light shade. Dormant in summer.

Primula (C) (semi-evergreen perennials)
SIZE: Dependent on variety; those mentioned below are 20 x 20cm (8 x 8in)
DESCRIPTION: *P. vulgaris* (primroses), with their pale yellow flowers, and *P. veris* (cowslips), a stronger yellow, are a must for the cottage garden, as are polyanthus. All are spring flowering.
CULTIVATION: Primroses need shade and a moist but well-drained soil. Cowslips need sun and are good on dry, limy soil. Polyanthus grow well in any fertile soil in sun.

Selinum wallichianum (herbaceous perennial)
SIZE: 90 x 60cm (3 x 2ft)
DESCRIPTION: Finely divided foliage and refined cow parsley-like heads make a truly graceful plant, which flowers in summer. *Myrrhis odorata* is very similar, if not quite so elegant.
CULTIVATION: Any reasonable soil; sun or full shade. Dislikes drought.

Trillium grandiflorum WAKE-ROBIN (herbaceous perennial)
SIZE: 45 x 45cm (1½ x 1½ft)
DESCRIPTION: Three-petalled flowers of purest white. A classic American woodland flower.
CULTIVATION: Shade and humus-rich, moist, but not wet, soil essential. Slow to establish.

PLANTS FOR WILD GARDENS:
TEMPERATE JUNGLES

Acacia (F, T) MIMOSA (evergreen trees and shrubs)
SIZE: Dependent on variety
DESCRIPTION: In Mediterranean countries, the

year starts with the scented, yellow flowers of *A. dealbata* (12 x 6m/40 x 20ft). Its feathery, dark green leaves give a distinctive look to the garden for the rest of the year. *A. pravissima* (5 x 5m/16 x 16ft) has angular foliage and a more compact habit, which is suitable for containers.
CULTIVATION: Just hardy, needing a sheltered site in full sun. Any well-drained soil. Rapid-growing and recovers quickly after frost damage.

Arundo donax (S) (deciduous grass)
SIZE: 3m x 90cm (10 x 3ft)
DESCRIPTION: Huge stems with grey-green foliage resembling sugar cane.
Cultivation: Fertile, preferably moist soil; full sun. Avoid cold areas.

Brugmansia (F, C, T) ANGELS' TRUMPETS (evergreen shrubs)
SIZE: 5 x 4m (16 x 13ft), in warm climates only
DESCRIPTION: Also known as datura, these shrubs have huge, pendent trumpets with the most heavenly scent imaginable. There are various similar species and varieties, most of them white, pale yellow or pink. All parts are poisonous.
CULTIVATION: Fast-growing, frost-tender shrubs, so need to be grown in large pots in colder climates and brought inside over the winter. They need full sun and heavy feeding, and should not be pruned until after they flower. Can be planted in very fertile soil in summer.

Callistemon citrinus (C, T) AUSTRALIAN BOTTLEBRUSH (evergreen shrub)
SIZE: 3 x 2.5m (10 x 8ft)
DESCRIPTION: Startling scarlet, 'bottlebrush' flowers turn heads in early summer; it is a shame that the season is so short, although the arching stems have a certain charm.
CULTIVATION: Any reasonable, well-drained soil. Hardy only in full sun in sheltered positions. Drought-tolerant.

Fatsia japonica (C) (evergreen shrub)
SIZE: 3 x 3m (10 x 10ft)
DESCRIPTION: Very large, glossy, hand-shaped leaves and strong growth make this a first-class hardy exotic. Heads of creamy flowers in autumn.
CULTIVATION: Any reasonable soil in sun or shade. Dislikes wind.

Gunnera (herbaceous perennials)
SIZE: 2 x 2.5m (6½ x 8ft)
DESCRIPTION: The vast rhubarb-like foliage of *G. manicata* brings the jungle (or dinosaurs) instantly to mind. *G. tinctoria* is only two-thirds the size. Both are classic waterside plants.
CULTIVATION: Fertile, wet soil. Cover with straw or similar in winter in cold areas.

Hosta (herbaceous perennials)
SIZE: 30–60 x 30–60cm (1–2 x 1–2ft)
DESCRIPTION: Large rosettes of bold leaves make hostas favourite plants for shade. *H.* 'Frances Williams' is an old yellow variegated one that has never been beaten. *H. sieboldiana* var. *elegans* is one of the most magnificent; huge pleated leaves with a blue-grey bloom. Most varieties have rather insignificant mauve flowers in summer.
CULTIVATION: Moist, but not waterlogged, soil in light shade is needed for satisfactory growth. Adored by slugs.

Macleaya (herbaceous perennials)
SIZE: 2.2 x 1.5m (7 x 5ft)
DESCRIPTION: Also known as *Bocconia*. Utterly magnificent grey-buff foliage of distinct and noble shape. Plumes of tiny white or coral flowers in

summer. *M. microcarpa* can be invasive; the practically identical *M. cordata* is not.
CULTIVATION: Any reasonable soil in sun or light shade. Good in moist soils.

Musa basjoo (C, T) JAPANESE, OR HARDY, BANANA (herbaceous perennial with persistent stem)
SIZE: 3m × 90cm (10 × 3ft)
DESCRIPTION: Metre-long, paddle-shaped leaves bring the tropics to mind like nothing else! Eventually produces (inedible) fruit.
CULTIVATION: Fertile and moist, well-drained soil in a sunny position sheltered from all wind. The roots are hardy but the stem should be protected from frost as much as possible, either by wrapping with bubble plastic or enclosing in a 'chimney' of terracotta flue liners packed with straw.

Palms (C) (evergreen trees)
SIZE: Dependent on species
DESCRIPTION: Quintessentially exotic. *Trachycarpus fortunei* (10 × 3m/33 × 10ft) is actually very hardy, and grows quite quickly. Other species are worth trying in warmer gardens or in containers.
CULTIVATION: Any reasonable soil in full sun. Dislike wind. Hardy to -14°C (7°F).

Pseudopanax (evergreen shrubs and small trees)
SIZE: 1.5–5 × 90cm–3m (5–16 × 3–10ft), depending on variety
DESCRIPTION: Elegant and rather exotic-looking hand-shaped foliage for tropical effects.
CULTIVATION: Any reasonable soil; full sun and shelter.

Rheum palmatum ORNAMENTAL RHUBARB (herbaceous perennial)
SIZE: 2 × 1.5m (6½ × 5ft)
DESCRIPTION: Huge, rhubarb-like leaves, often tinged a bronze-red. Dramatic, creamy flower spike in early summer.
CULTIVATION: Fertile, moist but not wet soil; full sun or light shade.

TREES

Acer palmatum (C) JAPANESE MAPLE (deciduous trees)
SIZE: Dependent on variety; slow growing
DESCRIPTION: Renowned for their beautiful hand-shaped leaves, autumn colour and zig-zag branching habit. Some, like *A. p.* 'Osakazuki', grow into small trees (5 × 5m/16 × 16ft). Others, e.g. *A. p.* var. *dissectum*, remain as dwarf hummocks (1.5 × 2m/5 × 6½ft).
CULTIVATION: Any reasonable soil that never dries out; shelter from wind. Sun or light shade.

Aralia DEVIL'S WALKING STICK (deciduous trees, shrubs, perennials)
SIZE: Dependent on variety
DESCRIPTION: Striking and sinister-looking plants with elegant, much-divided foliage, bunches of tiny, cream flowers in late summer and black berries. The shrub *A. elata* (3 × 3m/10 × 10ft) has an architectural, tree-like shape; *A. e.* 'Variegata' is a superior form. *A. cachemirica* (90 × 75cm/3 × 2½ft) is a herbaceous perennial with rounded foliage.
CULTIVATION: Any reasonable soil in sun or light shade.

Arbutus (C) STRAWBERRY TREE (evergreen trees)
SIZE: 8 × 8m (26 × 26ft)
DESCRIPTION: Peeling cinnamon bark and a sculptural habit give the Mediterranean evergreens *A. unedo* and *A.* × *andrachnoides* a magical

quality. White 'lily-of-the-valley' flowers and strawberry-like fruits.
CULTIVATION: Full sun and well-drained soil in sheltered localities. Good on thin limestone soils. *A. marina* is the fastest-growing.

Betula BIRCH (deciduous trees)
SIZE: Fast-growing, to 15 × 7m (50 × 23ft)
DESCRIPTION: Renowned for their silvery bark and hardiness, birches evoke the wild places of the north. Their shade is usefully light. *B. utilis* var. *jacquemontii* is a good upright grower with white bark, while *B. albosinensis* has buff-coloured bark.
CULTIVATION: Anywhere that avoids extremes of heat, drought or wet. Suitable for severe cold and exposure.

Catalpa INDIAN BEAN TREE (deciduous trees)
SIZE: 15 × 15m (50 × 50ft)
DESCRIPTION: Exotic-looking but fully hardy trees with large, heart-shaped leaves, bunches of white flowers in summer, and long, bean-like fruit.
CULTIVATION: Fertile, well-drained but moist soil; full sun.

Cercidiphyllum japonicum KATSURA (deciduous tree)
SIZE: 18 × 15m (60 × 50ft)
DESCRIPTION: A gracefully upright and fast-growing tree. The leaves are bronze in spring and a variety of colours in autumn.
CULTIVATION: Well-drained but constantly moist soils, especially acid ones; full sun.

Cupressus sempervirens (evergreen tree)
SIZE: Slow-growing, to 30 × 3m (100 × 10ft)
DESCRIPTION: The reed-thin cypress so typical of Mediterranean landscapes. Dark green foliage.
CULTIVATION: Any reasonable well-drained soil; full sun. Hardier than often thought, but avoid cold winds and frost pockets. Older trees are hardier.

Fruit trees
SIZE: Dependent upon rootstock used; dwarf varieties are commonly available
DESCRIPTION: Apple and pear trees can easily be fitted into a small space if they are grown as cordons or espaliered on to a wall. The correct rootstock must be chosen and a programme of careful pruning followed. Their pink or white spring flowers are also valuable. Plums, peaches and nectarines can be grown as espaliers on warm, sheltered walls.
CULTIVATION: Full sun; deep, fertile soil. Best bought from specialist nurseries.

Olea europaea (C, T) OLIVE (evergreen tree)
SIZE: 10 × 10m (33 × 33ft), in warm climates only
DESCRIPTION: Hardier than often supposed, the grey-leaved olive forms an attractive small tree. Fruit is unlikely except in warmer climates.
CULTIVATION: Needs a sheltered spot in full sun, e.g. against a wall. Good drainage essential.

Parrotia persica PERSIAN IRONWOOD (deciduous tree)
SIZE: 10 × 10m (33 × 33ft)
DESCRIPTION: A somewhat weeping habit and good autumn colour render this a desirable garden tree. Like all weeping trees, it makes a good hiding place.
CULTIVATION: Any reasonable soil in sun.

Paulownia tomentosa FOXGLOVE TREE
SIZE: 12 × 6m (40 × 20ft)
DESCRIPTION: Huge foliage, and (on older plants) bunches of purple-blue, foxglove-like flowers make this a truly exotic plant.

CULTIVATION: Easily frost damaged, although the roots are fully hardy. Best treated as a herbaceous foliage plant. Fertile soil and full sun.

Picea CHRISTMAS TREE, SPRUCE (evergreen trees)
SIZE: Dependent on variety
DESCRIPTION: Valued for their shape and character, the finest are *P. breweriana* (10 × 6m/33 × 20ft), with blue-tinged, pendent foliage, and *P. omorika* (15 × 5m/50 × 16ft) with its sombre beauty.
CULTIVATION: Any reasonable soil; full sun. *P. breweriana* can be slow to get going; *P. omorika* thrives on thin limestone soils and in urban areas.

Pinus PINE (evergreen trees)
SIZE: Dependent on variety; mostly around 20 × 10m (65 × 33ft)
DESCRIPTION: Laden with symbolic and spiritual meaning, pines include some of the most elegant and romantic of trees. *P. sylvestris* (Scots pine) develops into a fine, asymmetrical old tree, as does *P. densiflora*, the classic Japanese pine. *P. wallichiana* has shaggily long, soft needles; *P. patula* and other Mexican species have even more extravagantly long needles. *P. pinea* (stone pine) is the umbrella-shaped species of the Mediterranean.
CULTIVATION: Full sun and well-drained soil. Most are good on poor and dry soils.

Prunus CHERRY, PLUM (deciduous trees)
SIZE: Dependent on variety; those mentioned below are around 10 × 8m (33 × 26ft)
DESCRIPTION: White or pink flowers in spring, although the strong pinks are unpopular with many. Subtler are *P. sargentii* (pale pink), *P.* × *yedoensis* (blush-white), 'Ukon' (palest yellow) and 'Spire' (soft pink, narrow habit). Autumn colours are often quite spectacular.
CULTIVATION: Best in deep, fertile soils; full sun.

Pyrus salicifolia WEEPING, OR SILVER, PEAR (deciduous tree)
SIZE: 5 × 3m (16 × 10ft)
DESCRIPTION: With its silvery foliage on slightly weeping branches, the weeping pear resembles an olive tree. Can be trained into a more formal shape. White flowers in spring.
CULTIVATION: Sun; any reasonable soil.

Quercus OAK (evergreen or deciduous trees)
SIZE: Species mentioned below are slow-growing, to 12 × 8m (40 × 26ft)
DESCRIPTION: The common oak (*Q. robur*) is full of mystical significance and develops into a very sculptural old tree. The evergreen *Q. ilex* is a vital part of the Mediterranean scene.
CULTIVATION: *Q. robur* tolerates practically any soil, both wet and dry; full sun. *Q. ilex* needs any reasonable soil, full sun and some shelter.

Salix × ***sepulcralis*** var. ***chrysocoma*** WEEPING WILLOW (deciduous tree)
SIZE: 15 × 20m (50 × 65ft)
DESCRIPTION: The classic weeping tree; its curtains of pendent branches of yellowy leaves are perfect for hiding behind.
CULTIVATION: Full sun; fertile, preferably moist or wet soils.

Stewartia pseudocamellia (C) (deciduous shrub or small tree)
SIZE: Slow-growing, to 10 × 5m (33 × 16ft)
DESCRIPTION: White flowers in late summer. Good autumn colour and peeling cinnamon bark.
CULTIVATION: Deep, moist but well-drained, acid soil in light shade.

INDEX

Page numbers in *italic* refer to the illustrations

A

Acacia 110, 152
  A. baileyana 120, 122
  A. dealbata 117
  A. pravissima 117
Acanthus 45
Acer 147
  A. campestre 112
  A. griseum 68, 71
  A. palmatum 68, 71, 153
  A. platanoides 'Drummondii' 89
Actinidia 89
  A. deliciosa 63, 151
  A. kolomikta 82–5
Adiantum 149
  A. venustum 137
Aesculus x carnea 147
Agrostis 114
Akebia quinata 151
Alchemilla alpina 137
  A. conjuncta 137
  A. mollis 61, 137
American gardens 13, 26, 36, 42–5, 53, 81, 105
Anthriscus sylvestris 30
Antirrhinum 131
Aralia 153
arbours 49, 51, 53, 62, 66, 67, 139
Arbutus 153
arcades 75, 82
archways 36, 36
Arenga engleri 122
Aristolochia 64, 113
Arts and Crafts style 26, 37
Arundo donax 152
Asplenium scolopendrium 149
avenues 29
azaleas 97

B

Bac, Ferdinand 33
Bachelard, Gaston 37
Bacon, Francis 52, 64, 103
Badminton, Avon 53
bamboos 30, 42, 45, 71, 94, 97, 106, 117, 120, 120, 121, 135, 150
Bambusa glaucescens 42, 45
Barragán, Luis 93
Bastie d'Urfé 130
Bateman, James 26–7, 57
Bell, Quentin 105
belvederes 61
berberis 114
Betula 153
  B. pendula 67, 71, 112
Biddulph Grange, Staffordshire 26, 26–7, 36–7, 57
Bixby, Florence Green 26
Blickling Hall, Norfolk 32
Bomarzo, Rome 41, 128, 128
Bonnefont Cloister Herb Garden, New York 79
Borago officinalis 151
Borges, Jorge Luis 55
'borrowed' views 85
boscos 103, 128
bosquets 103
bowers 52, 62, 67, 131, 139
Bradley-Hole, Christopher 81
Bramham Park, Yorkshire 39
Breton, André 133
Brugmansia 131, 152
Buddleja alternifolia 93

B. davidii 150
Burnett, Frances Hodgson 30, 99
Burroughs, Edgar Rice 129
Buxus microphylla var. japonica 45, 97
  B. sempervirens 150

C

cacti 93
Caesalpinia gilliesii 45
Callistemon citrinus 57, 152
Camellia 150
Campanula 61
  C. rotundifolia 151
Cardamine pratensis 151
Cardiocrinum giganteum 113, 152
Carex comans 116
Carpenteria californica 63, 150
Carpinus betulus 150
Castle Howard, Yorkshire 53
Catalpa 97, 113, 153
  C. bignonioides 113
  C. speciosa 113
caves 126, 130, 137, 143
Ceanothus 150
Centaurea 151
Cephalaria gigantea 151
Cercidiphyllum japonicum 113, 153
Cercis siliquastrum 113
Chaerophyllum hirsutum 'Roseum' 30, 151
Chamaecyparis lawsoniana 33, 147
Chamaedorea radicalis 122
Chamaerops humilis 117
Charleston, East Sussex 105
cherry trees 45, 89, 144, 147, 153
Chimonanthus praecox 59, 149
Chinese gardens 13, 15, 17, 26, 30–2, 34–6, 55, 76–7, 82, 85, 87–9, 129
Choisya ternata 32, 43, 45, 71, 150
Church, Thomas 61, 110, 140
Chusan palm 117
Cistus 150
city gardens 74–94, 74–97
clearings 114–15
Clematis 56, 89, 151
  C. alpina 56, 67, 144, 147
  C. armandii 56, 67
  C. cirrhosa var. balearica 67
  C. x fargesioides 56
  C. florida 'Sieboldii' 85
  C. integrifolia 66
  C. montana 147
Clément, Gilles 107
climbers 63–4, 55–6, 82–5, 89, 151
Cliveden, Bucks 32, 110
cloister gardens 79
Colquhounia coccinea 63
coppices 113
Le Corbusier 81
Cornus 147
Cortaderia selloana 71
Corylus avellana 'Contorta' 57, 71
Cotinus coggygria Purpureus Group 71
  C. c. 'Royal Purple' 57
Cotoneaster 45
  C. lacteus 114
courtyards 13, 76–9, 76–9, 82–9, 88–9
crabapple, Japanese 45
Crataegus 147
  C. monogyna 112
Crocosmia masoniorum 45
Cupressus torulosa 'Cashmeriana' 122
  C. macrocarpa 45
  C. sempervirens 153

Cycas revoluta 122
Cyclamen 149
cypresses 45, 94, 96, 113, 144, 147
Cyrtomium falcatum 133
Cytisus battandieri 150

D

Dali, Salvador 128
Danckerts, Henry 104
Daphne 149
Dashwood, Sir Francis 52
Defoe, Daniel 129
dens 138–9, 138–9
Désert de Retz, Paris 53, 133
Dianthus 149
Dicksonia antarctica 117, 122
Dierama pulcherrimum 149
Digitalis 152
doorways 17, 30, 30–1, 32, 37, 148
Doré, Gustave 128
Dryopteris 152
  D. erythrosora 122
Duchêne, Achille 81
Dumbarton Oaks, Washington DC 26–7, 89

E

Eade, Belinda 143
Eames, Charles 109
Egypt, Ancient 12, 19, 50
Eichhornia crassipes 116
Elaeagnus 45
  E. commutata 94, 95, 97
  E. x ebbingei 97
Eliot, T.S. 15
entrances 30–2, 30–1
Escallonia 114, 147, 150
Eucalyptus nitens 122
euonymus 45
Euphorbia characias 135
  E. canariensis 84
  E. dulcis 'Chameleon' 135
  E. x martinii 135
Evelyn, John 14

F

Fagus sylvatica 67, 71
Fairbrother, Nan 77
Fallopia baldschuanica 57, 147
fan palms 117
fantasy 126–44, 126–47
Fargesia nitida 122
Farrand, Beatrix 26–7, 53
Fatsia japonica 137, 152
ferns 45, 94, 97, 133
Festuca 114
Ficus 71
Finlay, Ian Hamilton 12, 134–5
Fish, Margery 37
Fleming, Sir Daniel 51
follies 36, 52, 57, 133
Fortune, Robert 26
fountains 76, 83, 87
framing views 32
Fraxinus excelsior 67
Fremontodendron 'California Glory' 89
Fritillaria meleagris 114, 151
fruit trees 71, 153

G

Galanthus 149
Garrya elliptica 'Evie' 57
gates 30
gazebos 60–1, 61, 68
Generalife, Granada 42
Geranium 152
  G. pratense 151
giardino segreto 14, 17, 24–6, 24–5, 41

Ginkgo biloba 147
Girardin, Marquis de 104–5
gloriettes 15, 61
grasses 152
gravel gardens 86
Greece, Ancient 12, 19, 102, 130
Grizedale Forest, Cumbria 143
Groombridge Place, Kent 143
grottoes 127, 129–33, 132–3, 136–7, 143
groves 12, 103, 128
Gunnera 152
  G. manicata 117

H

Hadrian's Villa, Tivoli 39
Hadspen Garden, Somerset 33
Ham House, London 104
Hamilton, Charles 52, 130–3
Harbison, Robert 41, 130
Harris, Richard 143
Hedera 151
  H. helix 97
hedges 30, 33–5, 114
Hedychium 45
Heligan, Cornwall 39, 118–19
Hellbrunn, Austria 129
Hemerocallis fulva 119
Hepworth, Barbara 32–3
herbs 29, 79, 97
Het Loo 53, 57
Hicks, Ivan 143
hideaways 138–9, 138–9
The Hill Garden, London 63
Hofmannsthal, Hugo von 89
Holboellia coriacea 122
holly 43, 45, 71, 112
hops 56, 144, 147
Hortus Conclusus 77
Hosta 152
Hoya australis 89
Humulus lupulus 147
Hydrangea petiolaris 137
Hyoscyamus niger 149

I

Iford Manor, Wiltshire 77
Ilex 110
  I. aquifolium 45, 71, 112
Impatiens balsamina 94
Iris 151–2
Islamic gardens 13, 14, 50, 76, 82, 87
Itoh, Teiji 85

J

Japanese gardens 14, 76, 82, 85, 86, 87, 92–3, 129
Jardin des Colombières, Menton 33
Jarman, Derek 17, 86
Jasminum 64, 89, 151
  J. officinale 56
Jeanneret, Pierre 81
Jekyll, Gertrude 26, 53, 61, 62, 64, 113, 138
Jellicoe, Sir Geoffrey 17, 32, 76
Johnson, Dr 130
Jones, Inigo 129
jungles 116–23, 117–20, 152–3
Juniperus communis 112
  J. x pfitzeriana 45
  J. rigida 113
  J. scopulorum 'Skyrocket' 97
  J. squamata 122

K

Kent, William 67, 104, 104
Keswick, Maggie 85
Klee, Paul 32
Kröller-Müller sculpture park 12–13

L
labyrinths 128
Lachryma Montis, California 53
landscape gardens 104–5
Lavandula 149
Leonardo da Vinci 129–30
Leverhulme, Lord 63
Ligularia stenocephala 111
Ligustrum japonicum 122
Lilium 149
Linderhof, Bavaria 67, 130
Lodge, David 34
Long Barn, Kent *30*
Lonicera 151
    L. japonica 'Halliana' 56
    L. periclymenum 56
    L. sempervirens 56
Lutyens, Sir Edwin 53
Lymonothamnus floribundus 122

M
Macleaya 152–3
Magnolia 45
    M. stellata 149
Mahonia 71
    M. lomariifolia 122
Malus 97, 147
    M. floribunda 45
Mandragora officinarum 149
Masson, Georgina 24
Mather, Rick *90*, 92
Mawson, Thomas 63
mazes 128, *129*, 140
meadows 109, 114–15, *114–15*, 151–2
Meconopsis cambrica 113
Medici, Duke Francesco de' 129
Medieval gardens 77, 102
Miller, Naomi 136
miradors 61
mirrors 89, *127*
Miscanthus sacchariflorus 97
    M. sinensis 'Variegatus' 59
Mogul dynasty 15, 129
monasteries 79
moon doors and windows 85
Moorish gardens 82, 87
Morus alba 67, 68, 71
moss 152
Muehlenbeckia complexa 15
Muller, Camille 87, 94
Munstead Wood, Surrey 26, 61
Musa basjoo 117, 153
Myosotis 149
Myrrhis odorata 113
Myrtus communis 149

N
Nephrolepis exaltata 133
Nerium oleander 94, 96, 97
Nicolson, Harold 27, 61, 114
Ninfa 30
Nymans, Sussex 67

O
oak trees 109, 110, 153
Olea europaea 153
Olmsted, Frederick Law 53
Omphalodes cappadocica 113
Onopordum nervosum 70, 71
Orsini, Count 41, 128, *128*
Osmanthus x burkwoodii 150
Osmunda regalis 107, 117

P, Q
Pacific Palisades, California 109
Page, Russell 10, 32, 57, 93
Painshill Park, Surrey 53, *53*,
    127, 130–3

Painswick Rococo Garden,
    Gloucestershire 53, *53*
Palazzo Farnese, Caprarola 24–6, 41
palm trees *78–9*, 153
Papaver rhoeas 152
paradise gardens 50, 76
Parc André-Citroën, Paris 107
Parrotia persica 113, 153
Parthenocissus 151
    P. henryana 64
    P. quinquefolia 91, 97, 147
Passiflora caerulea 64, 151
paths 17, *17–19*, 28, 37–9
Paulownia tomentosa 153
pavilions 50, 52, *54–5*, 55, 57, 59, *60*
paving materials 87–9
Paz, Octavio 93
pear trees 67, 71, 153
pelargoniums 94, 97
pergolas 53, 62–4, 67, 85
Philadelphus 150
Phyllostachys aurea 122
    P. bambusoides 106, 122, *123*
    P. nigra 97, 117, 122
Phymatosoros diversifolius 122
Picasso, Pablo 17, 33
Picea 153
    P. breweriana 113
Pileostegia viburnoides 56
Pinus (pine trees) 113, 153
    P. mugo 113
    P. nigra 122
    P. patula 113
    P. pinea 113
    P. radiata 122
    P. sylvestris 112
Pittosporum 43, 45, 150
pleached trees 29

plum trees 45, 153
Polianthes tuberosa 149
Pollan, Michael 17, 114, 148
Polygonatum multiflorum 152
Polystichum setiferum 137, 149
ponds 42, *42–3*, 82, 87
Pope, Alexander 17, 130
Primula 152
Prunus 45, 147, 153
    P. cerasifera 112
    P. 'Ukon' 71
Pseudopanax 153
    P. crassifolius 117
    P. ferox 117
Pyrus salicifolia 67, 71, 153
Quercus 153
    Q. ilex 32

R
Rabbitz, Carl 79
Rambouillet 129
Rancho Los Alamitos, California 26
Renaissance 14, 24, 79, 103, 128,
    129, 130, 134
retreats 48–68, *48–71*
Reynell, Diana 143
Rheum palmatum 153
Rhododendron 30, *43*, 45, 71, *101*, 150
Rhus typhina 71, 97, 147
Ribes 150
Ricinus communis 116
Robinia hispida 110
Robinson, William 105, 113
'Robinson parks' 129
Rome, Ancient 50, 130
roof gardens 75, 79–81, *80–1*,
    90–4, *90–7*
'rooms' 22–42, *22–45*
Rosa (roses) 32, 55–6, *61*, 63–4, 97,

113, 144, 150, 151
    R. banksiae 59
    R. 'Cécile Brunner' 42, 45, 56
    R. eglanteria 45
    R. 'Mme Alfred Carrière' 56
    R. moyesii 107
    R. mulliganii 56
    rosa mundi 17
    R. 'Nevada' 147
    R. 'New Dawn' *146*, 147
    R. 'Princesse de Nassau' *110*
    R. rubiginosa 114
Rousham, Oxfordshire 67, *104*
Rousseau, Jean-Jacques 104–5
ruins 30
Rydal Hall, Cumbria 51
Rydal Mount, Cumbria 39, *50–1*, 51

S
Sackville-West, Vita 27, *30*, 36, 87,
    114
Saint Laurent, Yves *84*
Salix 97, 147
    S. babylonica 67, 113
    S. caprea 'Kilmarnock' 67
    S. exigua 93
    S. x *sepulcralis* var. *chrysocoma*
    67, 113, 153
Sambucus racemosa 57, 135
Sarcococca 149
    S. hookeriana 79
Sartre, Jean-Paul 139
Schama, Simon 102
Schisandra rubriflora 63
screens 30, 85, 92, 150
sculpture 134–5
Selinum wallichianum 152
Semiarundinaria fastuosa 94, 97
shrubberies 29
Sissinghurst Castle, Kent 27, 36, 61,
    87, *112*, 113, 114
Solanum crispum 'Glasnevin' 93
Soleirolia soleirolii 116, *133*
    S. s. 'Aurea' *116*
Solenopsis fluviatilis 45
Sorbus aria 147
    S. aucuparia 112
    S. cashmiriana 71
    S. 'Joseph Rock' 71
spruce trees 113, 153
staircases 144, *141*, *146*
stepping stones 39, *134–5*
steps 14–15
Stewartia pseudocamellia 89,
    113, 153
Stipa 152
    S. gigantea 59
Stourhead, Wiltshire *132*
streams 116
Styrax abaxsia 71
sumach 71, 147
summerhouses *50–1*, 51, 53, 55–9,
    58–9, 68, *136–7*
sunken gardens 29, *37*
surprise 17, 36–7, *117*
Surrealists 133
sweet briar 114
Swiss Garden, Bedfordshire *49*, 61
Symphoricarpos 71
Syringa 71, 147

T
Tamarix ramosissima 57
    T. tetrandra 57
Tatton Park, Cheshire *52*
Taxus baccata 57, 112, *129*, 150
tea-gardens 76
tea-houses *52*, 53

temperate jungles *116–23*, 117–20,
    152–3
tender plants 119
Thalictrum 152
    T. rochebruneanum 30
Thamnocalamus crassinodus 122
Thijsse, Jacques P. 107
Thoreau, Henry David 105
Thymus 149
Tilia 67, 71
Tomlinson, Charles 139
topiary 127, *130*
town gardens 29, 74–94, *74–97*
Trachelospermum 89, 151
    T. asiaticum 63
    T. jasminoides 56
Trachycarpus fortunei 117, 122
    T. martianus 122
    T. oreophilus 122
    T. wagnerianus 122
treehouses 14, 129, 138, 140, *140–3*
trees 29, *29*, 67, 89, 110–13,
    110–13, 153
trellis *13*, 82, 92
Trillium grandiflorum 152
Trithrinax acanthocoma 122
trompe-l'oeil 57, 89, 127, 134–5
tufa 137
tunnels and tunnel-arbours 29, 30,
    62, *62–3*, 64–7, *70*
turf huts 68, *69*, *138–9*

U, V
urban gardens 74–94, *74–97*
Versailles 103, 130
Viburnum 150
    V. lantana 114
Villa Aldobrandini, Frascati 41
Villa Capponi, Florence 24
Villa d'Este, Rome 24, *24*, 128
Villa Gamberaia, Tuscany *24–5*
Villa Giulia, Rome 130
Villa Noailles, Grasse *16*
vines 45, 56, 64, 94, 147, 151
Viola 149–50
Vitis 147, 151
    V. coignetiae 97

W
walkways 144, *111–7*
walls 30, 32–3, 82, 85
Walpole, Horace 102–3
water 17–19, 42, *42–3*, *76*, *82*, *87*,
    93, *116*, 129, 134–5, *134*
Westminster Abbey, London *76*, 79
Westpark, Munich 107, 115
wicker *32*, *138*
wild-flower meadows 107, 109,
    114–15, *114–15*, 151–2
wild gardens 100–20, *100–23*, 151–2
wildernesses 15, 103–5
willows 64, 67, 93, 97, 113, 139,
    147, 153
wind, roof gardens 92
windows 85, *136–7*
Wirtz, Jacques 30
Wisteria 64, *131*, 144, 147, 151
woodland gardens *107*, 110–13,
    110–13, 152
Woolridge, John 51–2
Wordsworth, William 51
Wright, Thomas 51, 53
Wyss, J.R. 129

Y, Z
Yucca 120, *121*
    Y. aloifolia 122
Zen gardens *86*, 93

ACKNOWLEDGEMENTS

The Publisher would like to thank the following photographers and organizations for permission to reproduce the photographs in this book:
1 Fritz von der Schulenburg/The Interior Archive (designers: John Stefanidis/Arabella Lennox-Boyd); 2 Helen Fickling (designer: Jason de Grellier Payne); 3 Michelle Lamontagne/The Garden Picture Library/Mount Koya, Japan; 4 left Jerry Harpur/Penny Mill, Chelmsford, Essex; 4 right Gary Rogers/Casa do Campo, Portugal; 5 left Ron Sutherland/The Garden Picture Library (designer: Anthony Paul); 5 centre Michele Lamontagne/The Garden Picture Library; 5 right Sunniva Harte/The Enchanted Forest, Groombridge Place (designer: Ivan Hicks); 6 Tim Street-Porter/Val Verde – Montecito; 7 Hugh Palmer/Higham Court, Glos; 10 left Carlos Navajas/La Casa de Marie Claire; 10–11 Jerry Harpur/Crowninshields, Wilmington, Delaware, USA; 12 P. Tinslay/Vogue Entertaining, Australia; 13 Brigitte Thomas/The Garden Picture Library; 14–15 Gary Rogers/Pavlovsk, nr Petersburg, Russia; 16 Marianne Majerus/Villa Noailles; 17 Ursel Borstell/Jan van Summere, Netherlands; 18 Fritz von der Schulenburg/The Interior Archive (designers: John Stefanidis/Arabella Lennox-Boyd); 20 Jerry Harpur/Penny Mill, Chelmsford, Essex; 21 P. Tinslay/Australian Vogue Entertaining; 24 left Michele Lamontagne/Villa d'Este, Tivoli, Italy; 24–5 Gary Rogers/Villa Gambera, nr Florence, Italy; 26–7 Hugh Palmer (Biddulph Grange, Staffs); 28 Ken Druse; 29 Marianne Majerus/The Clock House, Wilts; 30 left Mr and Mrs Gough/Long Barn, Kent; 30 right John Glover/Toad Hall, Berks; 31 Jerry Harpur/Hazleby House, Berks; 32 Marianne Majerus; 33 Anne Hyde/Clapton Court, Somerset; 34–5 Ralf Turander/Jahres Zeiten Verlag/Architekther Wohnen; 36 left Andrew Lawson (designer: David Hicks); 36 right Ianthe Ruthven (John Last's Garden, Norfolk); 37 Gary Rogers (designer/owner: Andre' Schoellen, Luxembourg); 38–9 Ursel Borstell/Hazelby House; 40 Hugh Palmer/Palacio Viana, Cordoba, Spain; 41 Ursel Borstell/Pam and Nick Coote, Oxon; 42–5 Sandra Ivany/Barbara Chevalier's garden, California USA; 46 Gary Rogers/Casa do Campo, Portugal; 47 Anne Hyde/Swiss Garden, Beds; 50–1 Nick Meers/The Garden Picture Library/Rydal Mount, Ambleside, Cumbria; 52 Eric Crichton/Tatton Park (National Trust); 53 left Georges Leveque/Painshill Park, Surrey; 53 right Christopher Gallagher/The Garden Picture Library/Painshill Rococo Gardens; 54–5 Gary Rogers/The Garden Picture Library; 56 Steven Wooster/The Garden Picture Library/Titiki Point, Taihape, New Zealand; 57 Marianne Majerus; 58 Hugh Palmer/Little Onn Hall, Staffs; 59 left Mark Bolton/Chrissy Price, Somerset; 59 right Marianne Majerus/Walton Manor, Northumb; 60 Sunniva Harte/Somerset Lodge; 61 Marianne Majerus/The Little Cottage, Hants; 62 left Gary Rogers/Ida's Valley Homestead (owner/designer: Maj Philip Erskine); 62 right Gary Rogers/Villa Monestro Tessin, Switzerland; 63 left Eric Crichton/Mrs Spencer York Gate, Leeds; 63 right Fritz von der Schulenburg/The Interior Archive (designers: John Stefanidis/Arabella Lennox-Boyd); 64–5 Andrew Lawson (designer: John Miller); 66 Juliette Wade/Mr and Mrs Ranwell, Stanford, Dingley, Berks; 67 Christopher Simon Sykes/The Interior Archive; 68 Sunniva Harte/Chauffeur's Flat, Tandridge, Kent; 69 Jane Legate/The Garden Picture Library/Chauffeur's Flat, Tandridge, Kent; 70 right Sunniva Harte/Chauffeur's Flat, Tandridge, Kent; 71 top Jennifer Potter/Chauffeur's Flat, Tandridge, Kent; 71 bottom Sunniva Harte/Chauffeur's Flat, Tandridge, Kent; 72 Ron Sutherland/The Garden Picture Library (designer: Anthony Paul); 73 Gary Rogers/garden from Maria Joao de Mello, Portugal; 76 Neil Jinkerson/Jarrold Publishing/Westminster Abbey Cloister Garden, London; 77 Hugh Palmer/Jardines de las Reales Alcazares; 78–9 Annette Schreiner/Patio Andalou, Seville; 80 Christopher Wesnofske (architect: Peter Dewitt); 81 John Miller/The Garden Picture Library/ Kensington Roof Garden, London; 82 Roland Beaufre/Agence Top/Boccara, Marrakesh; 83 Jean Pierre Godeaut/Nourissa; 84 Annette Schreiner/Majorelle, Marrakesh; 85 Anne Tack/Verne Fotografie; 86 Marijke Heuff/The Garden Picture Library/Zen Buddhist Garden, Daitokusi, Kyoto; 87 Camille Muller, Paris; 88 Gary Rogers/Perth, Australia (owner/designer: Gary Banham); 89 Marianne Majerus (designer: Michele Osborne); 90 left Niall McDiarmid (designer: Rick Mather); 90–1 Georges Leveque (designer: Camille Muller); 92–3 Gary Rogers/Starnberg, Germany (owner/designer: Dietrich Muller); 93 right Marianne Majerus (designer/ceramics: Kenny Menczer); 94 Michele Lamontagne (designer: Camille Muller); 95 Camille Muller, Paris; 96 top Claire de Virieu/Inside, (designer: Camille Muller); 96 bottom Claire de Virieu (designer: Camille Muller); 97 Claire de Virieu (designer: Camille Muller); 98 Michele Lamontagne/The Garden Picture Library; 99 Mark Bolton/ Trevarno Estate and Gardens, Cornwall (owner: M. R. Sagin); 102–3 Gary Rogers/Villa Garzonoi, nr Florence, Italy; 103 right Andrew Lawson/Private Garden, Maine, USA; 104 Marianne Majerus/Rousham, Oxon; 105 Ianthe Ruthven/Charleston House, Sussex; 106–7 Ken Druse/Blithewold Gardens and Arboretum, Bristol, Rhode Island; 107 right Mark Bolton/Trevano Estate and Gardens, Corn, (owner: M. R. Sagin); 108 Gary Rogers/Perth, Australia. (owner/designer: Gary Banham); 109 Gary Rogers (owner/designer: Gerda Zwickel, Germany); 110 left Marianne Majerus; 110–11 Andrew Lawson/ private garden, Quebec, Canada; 112 Georges Leveque/Sissinghurst Castle, Kent; 113 Clay Perry/The Garden Picture Library/New Zealand; 114 left Susan Whitney; 114–15 Andrew Lawson (Courtesy of Miriam Rothshild); 116 Annette Schreiner; 117 Marianne Majerus/Hever Castle, Kent; 118–19 Andrea Jones/Heligan Gardens, Cornwall; 119 right Ken Druse/Dr Sumner Freedman, Fire Island, New York; 120–3 Helen Fickling (designer: Jason de Grellier Payne); 124 Sunniva Harte/The Enchanted Forest, Groombridge Place (designer: Ivan Hicks); 125 Jerry Harpur/Painshill Park; 128 Christina Gascoigne/Robert Harding Picture Library/Bomarzo, Villa Orsini, Viterbo, Italy; 129 Maurizio Borgese/Agence Top; 130 Gary Rogers/Villa Gamberia, nr Florence, Italy; 131 Ken Druse/Mohonk Mountain House, New Paltz, New York; 132 John Glover/NTPL/Stourhead, Wilts; 133 left Hugh Palmer/Marlborough, 133 right Mark Fiennes/Arcaid (designer: Ernest Newton); Wilts; 134 left Julia Brown/Edifice/Villa D'Este, Tivoli; 134–5 Clive Boursnall/Country Life Magazine, Little Sparta (designer: Ian Hamilton Finlay); 135 right Michele Lamontagne (designer: Sonny Garcia); 136–7 Marianne Majerus/Kingstone Cottages, Hereford (designer: Michael Hughes); 138 left Sunniva Harte/The Enchanted Forest, Groombridge Place; 138–9 Andrew Lawson/Cannwood Farm, Somerset; 139 right Brigitte Perdereau; 140 left Juliette Wade/The Farrells, Northants; 140 right William B. Steele/Mattiello Steele Associates; 141 Richard Waite/Arcaid (designer: Mark Wilkinson – Furniture maker); 142–3 Andrew Lawson; 143 right Marianne Majerus/Colombe D'Or; 144–7 Sunniva Harte/courtesy Mr and Mrs Mercy; 148 Marie O'Hara/Elizabeth Whiting & Associates/Longwood Farm, Glos.

The Author and Publisher would like to thank the following for permission to reproduce extracts in this book:
10, 32, 57 Russell Page: *The Education of a Gardener* (First published William Collins Sons & Co. Ltd., 1962) Copyright © the Executors of the Estate of Russell Page 1994, reproduced by permission of The Harvill Press
15 T. S. Eliot: 'Burnt Norton' *The Four Quartets* from *Collected Poems 1909–1962* (Faber and Faber UK/Brace, Harcourt, Javinovich USA)
17 Sir Geoffrey Jellicoe: *The Studies of a Landscape Designer over 80 Years*, Vols II & III (Garden Art Press, 1993)
17 Derek Jarman: *Derek Jarman's Garden* (Thames and Hudson, 1995)
17, 148 Michael Pollan: *Second Nature* (Bloomsbury Publishing Plc, 1996/ Reproduced in the US and Canada by permission of Grove Atlantic)
24 Georgina Masson: *Italian Gardens* (First published Thames and Hudson, 1961/revised edition Antique Collectors' Club, 1987)
87 *Vita Sackville-West's Garden Book* (Michael Joseph, 1968) Copyright © The Estate of Vita Sackville-West, reproduced by permission of Curtis Brown, London
34 David Lodge: *The Art of Fiction* (Penguin Books, 1992)
37 Gaston Bachelard: *The Poetics of Space* (Beacon Press, 1969)
41, 130 Robert Harbison: *Eccentric Spaces* (André Deutsch, 1977)
55 Jorge Luis Borges: *Ficciones* (Weidenfeld and Nicolson, 1992 UK/Grove Atlantic USA)
61 Gertrude Jekyll: *Arts and Crafts Gardens* (Antique Collectors' Club UK, 1981); originally published as *Gardens for Small Country Houses* (with Lawrence Weaver) (Country Life, 1912)
62 Gertrude Jekyll: *Wood and Garden* (First published Longmans, Green, and Co., 1899/new edition Antique Collectors' Club)
76 Cristiana Moldi-Ravenna and Tudy Sammartini: *Secret Gardens in Venice* (Arsenale Editrice Venice, 1996)
77 Nan Fairbrother: *Men and Gardens* (The Hogarth Press, London, 1956)
81 Dorothée Imbert: *The Modernist Garden in France* (Yale University Press, 1993)
85 Teiji Itoh: *Space and Illusion in the Japanese Garden* (Weatherhill, 1973)
93 Octavio Paz: 'Stanzas for an Imaginary Garden' *The Oxford Book of Garden Verse* ed. John Dixon Hunt (Oxford University Press, 1993)
102 Simon Schama: *Landscape and Memory* (Harper Collins Publishers Ltd., 1995, UK/The Peters Fraser and Dunlop Group Ltd. USA)
110 Thomas D. Church et al.: *Gardens are for People* (First published University of California Press, Berkeley, 1955; 3rd edition 1995) Copyright © 1983 Elizabeth R. Church.
114 Harold Nicolson's letter to his wife, Vita Sackville-West in Jane Brown: *Sissinghurst: Portrait of a Garden* (Weidenfeld and Nicolson, London, 1990)
136 Naomi Miller: *Heavenly Caves* (George Allen & Unwin, London,1982)
137 Barbara Jones: *Follies & Grottoes* (Constable, revised edition 1974)
139 Jean-Paul Sartre, translated by John Dixon Hunt: *The Oxford Book of Garden Verse* (Oxford University Press, 1993) by permission of Oxford University Press

As well as the above, background material can be found in: Geoffrey and Susan Jellicoe, Patrick Goode, Michael Lancaster (eds), *The Oxford Companion to Gardens* (Oxford University Press, 1986); David C. Streatfield, *California Gardens: creating a new Eden* (Abbeville Press); Maggie Keswick, *The Chinese Garden*, 2nd revised edition (Academy Editions, 1986).

The Author gives special thanks to Stuart Cooper, Kate Bell, Isabel de Cordova, Helen Fickling and Tanya Robinson for all their help and inspiration. Thanks are also due to Barbara Chevalier, Jason de Grellier Payne, Mr and Mrs Mercy, Camille Muller, and Mr and Mrs Richins for so kindly allowing us to photograph their gardens. And finally to Rachel Hagan, Catherine Lamontagne, Tony Lord and Sarah Widdecombe.